FUN AND CHALLENGING
MAZES
FOR KIDS 8-12

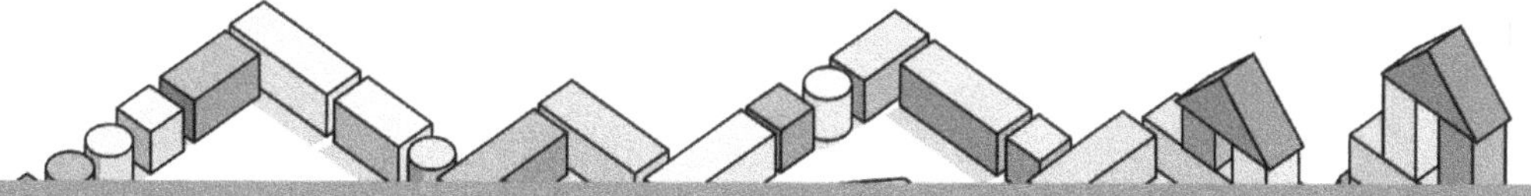

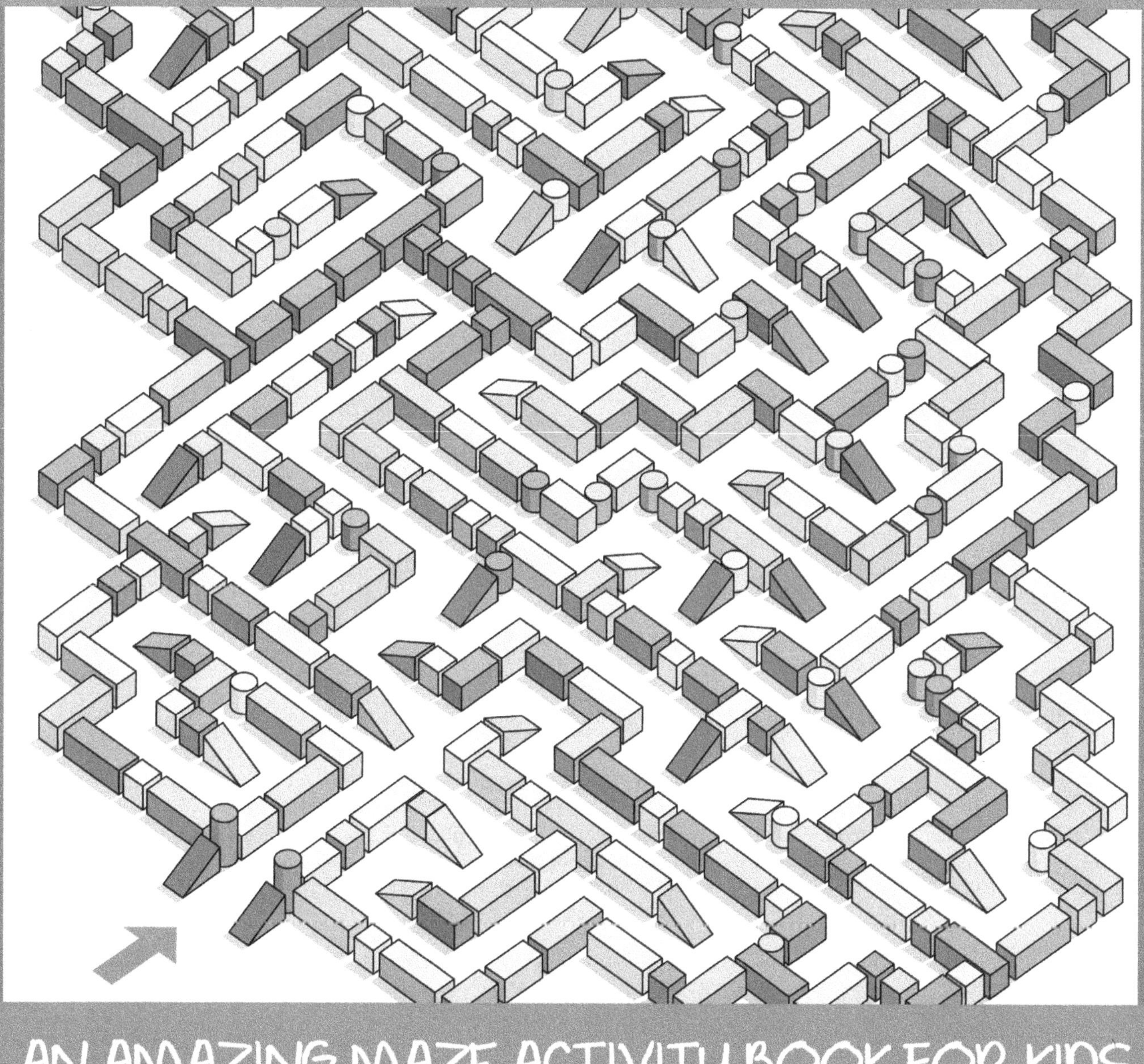

AN AMAZING MAZE ACTIVITY BOOK FOR KIDS

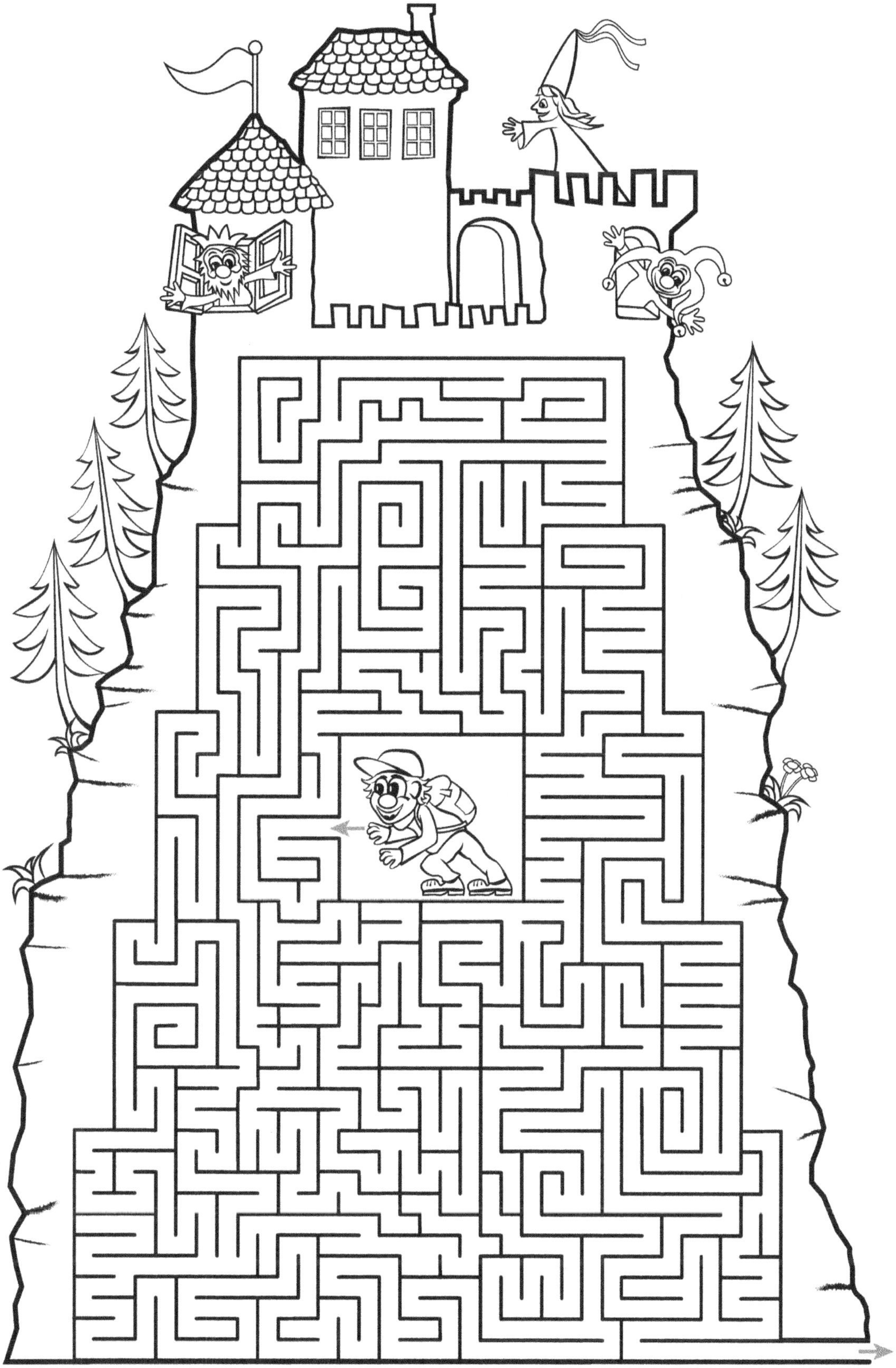

2

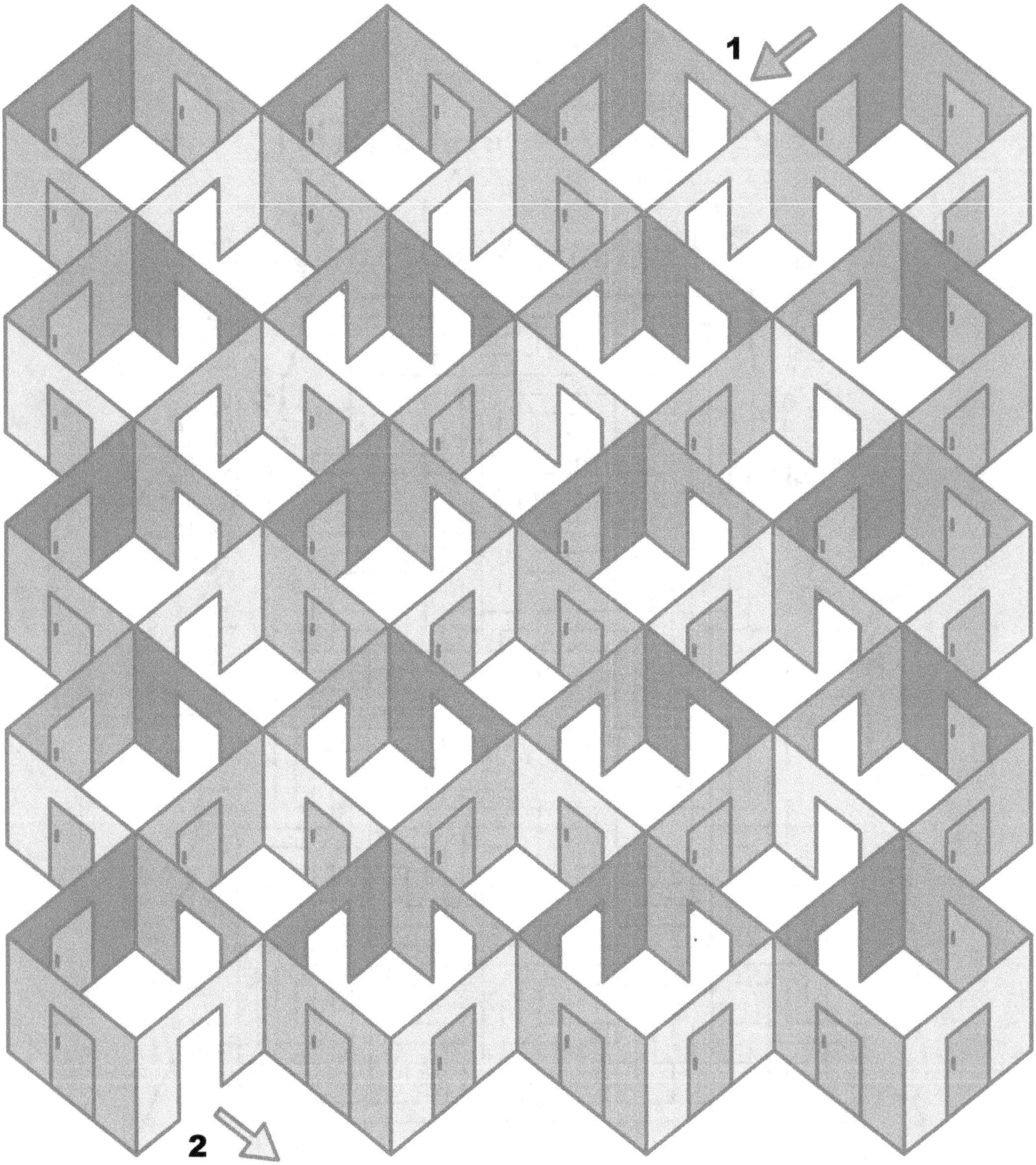

1
2

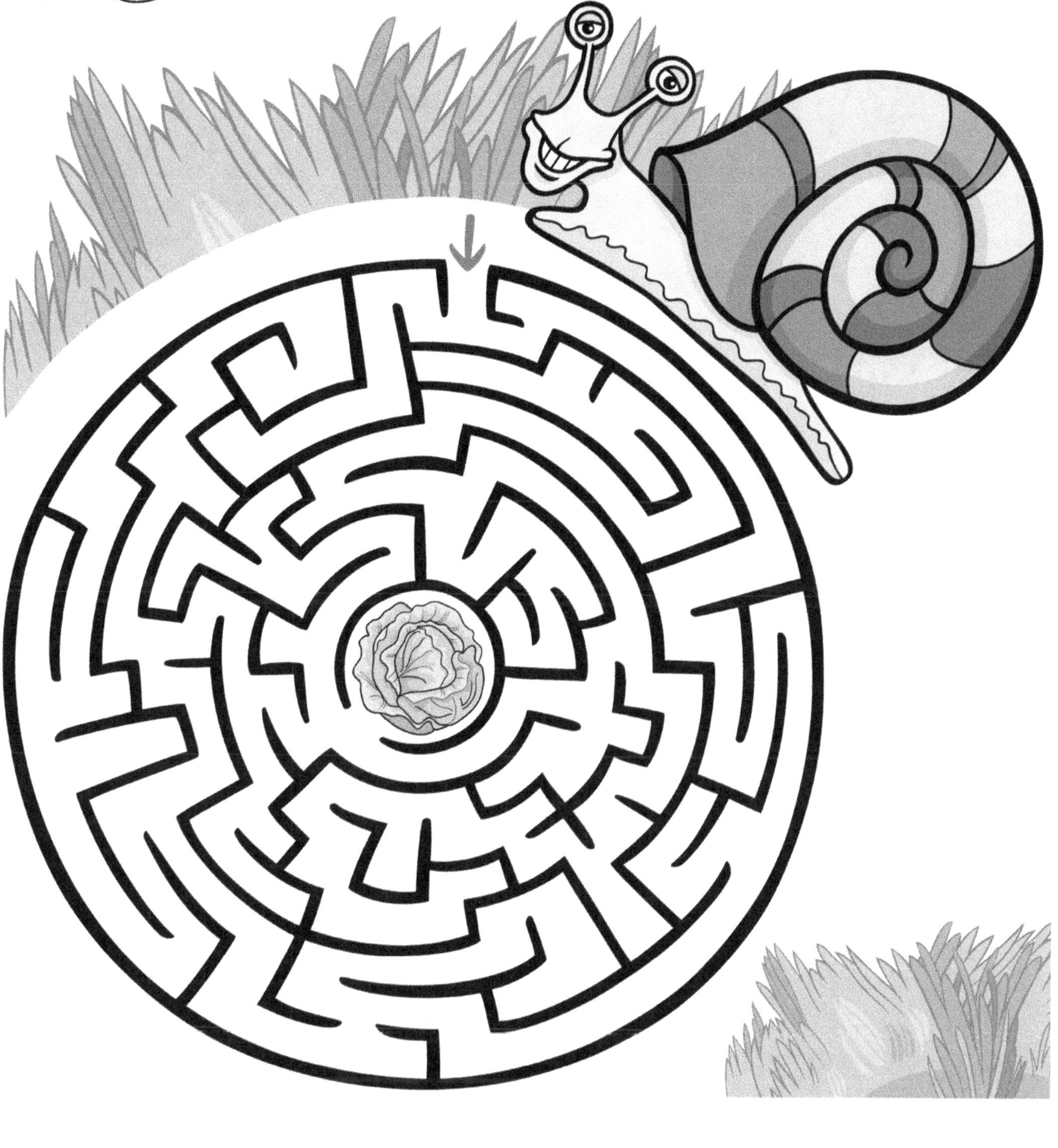

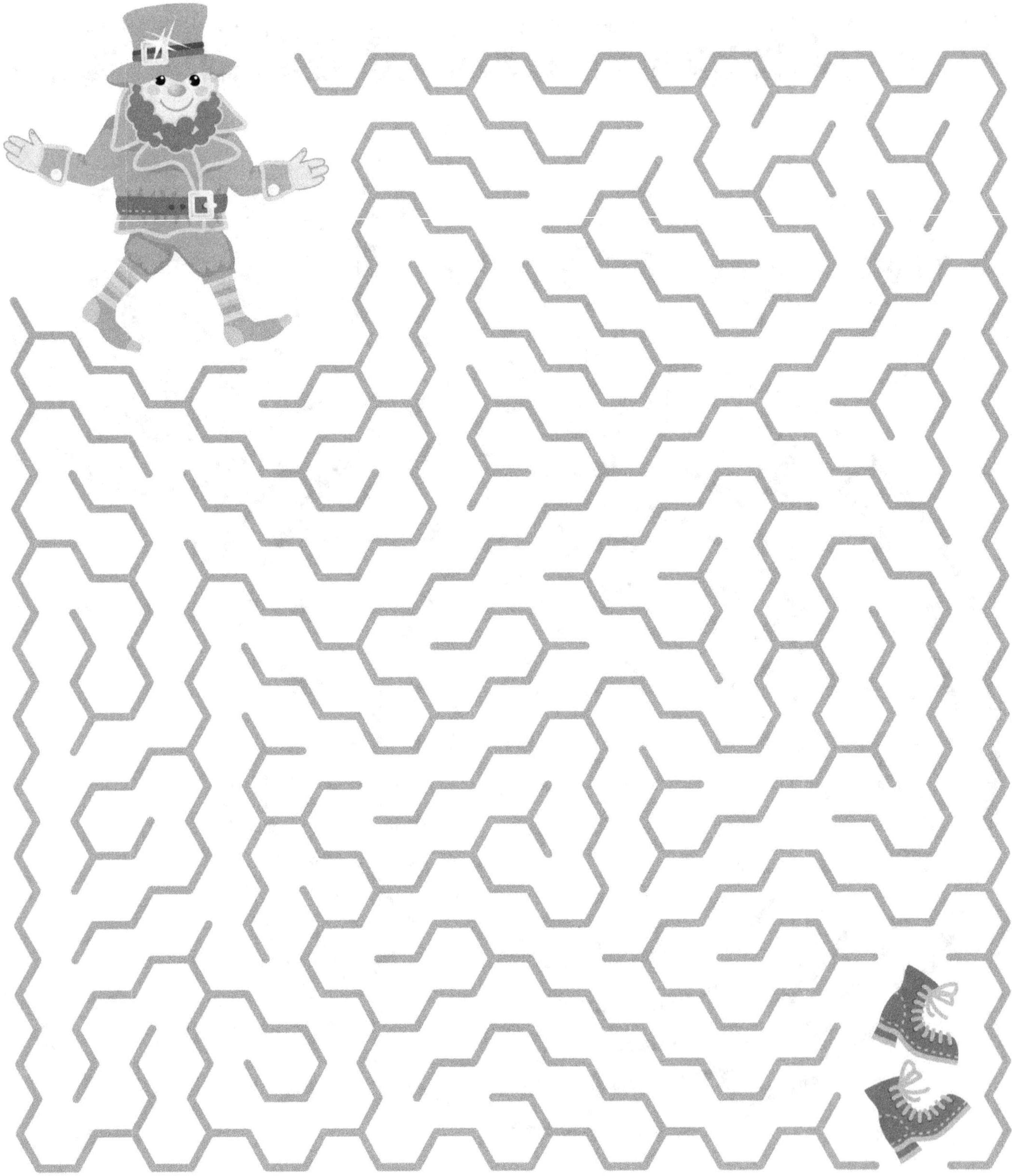

5

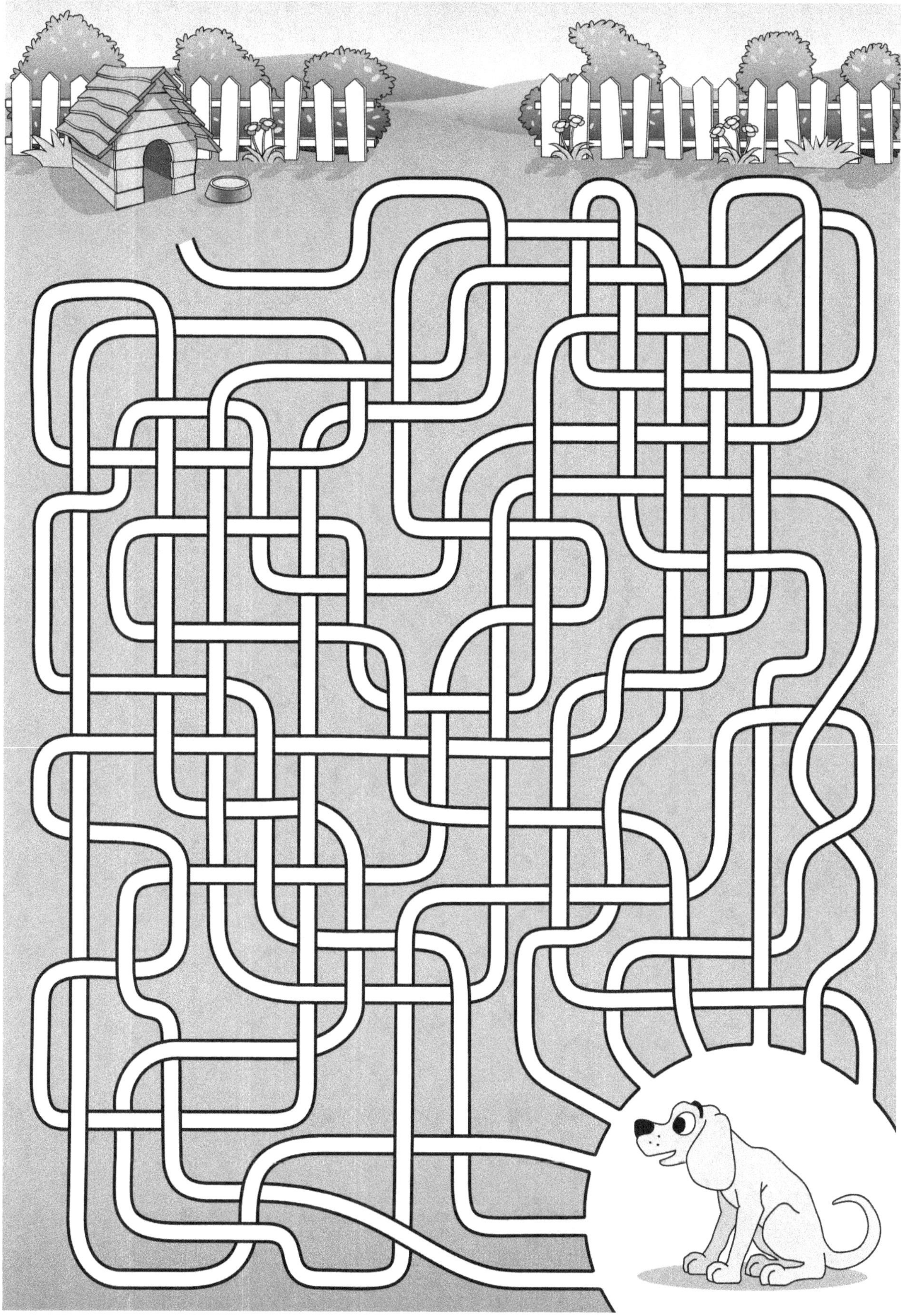

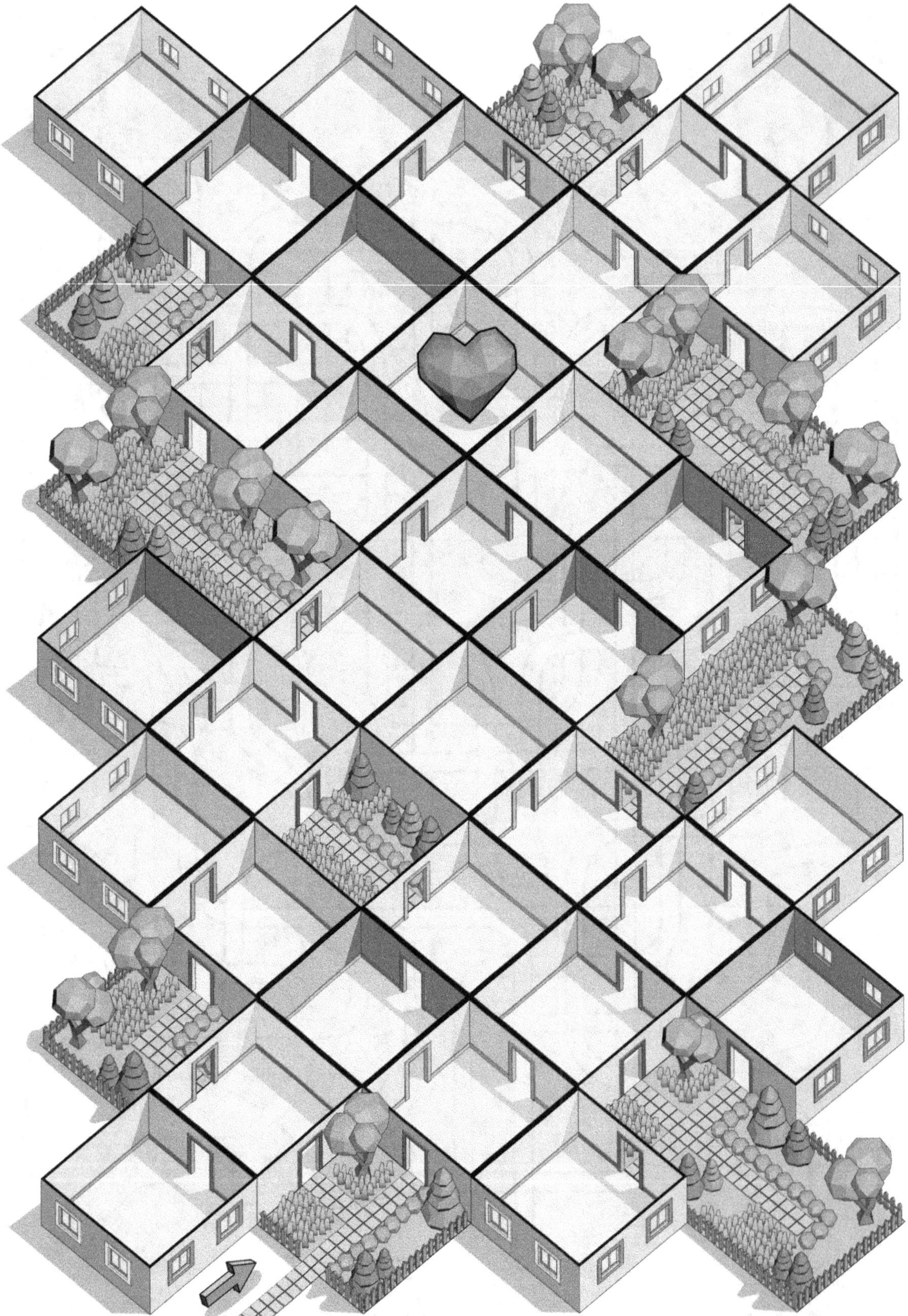

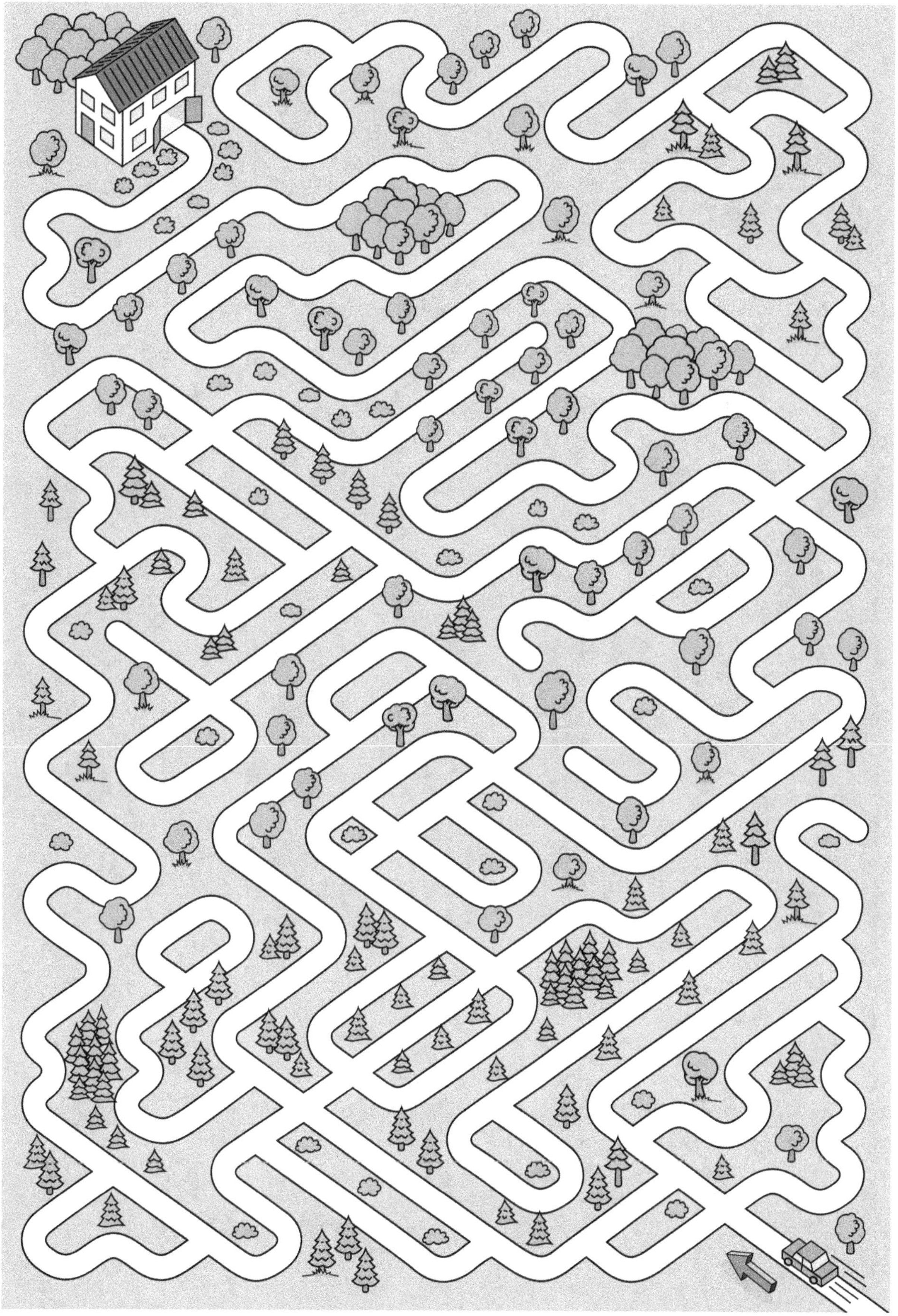

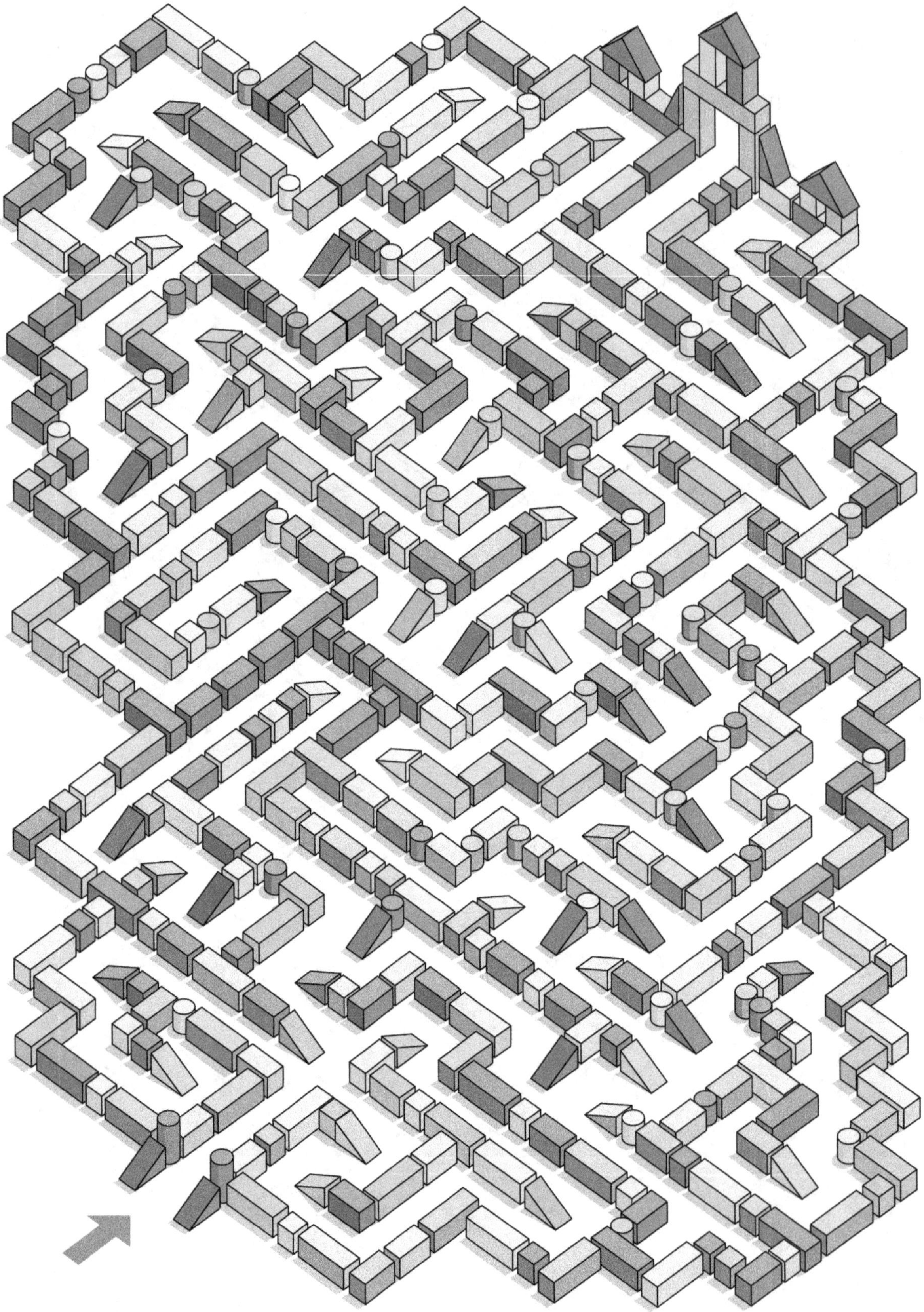

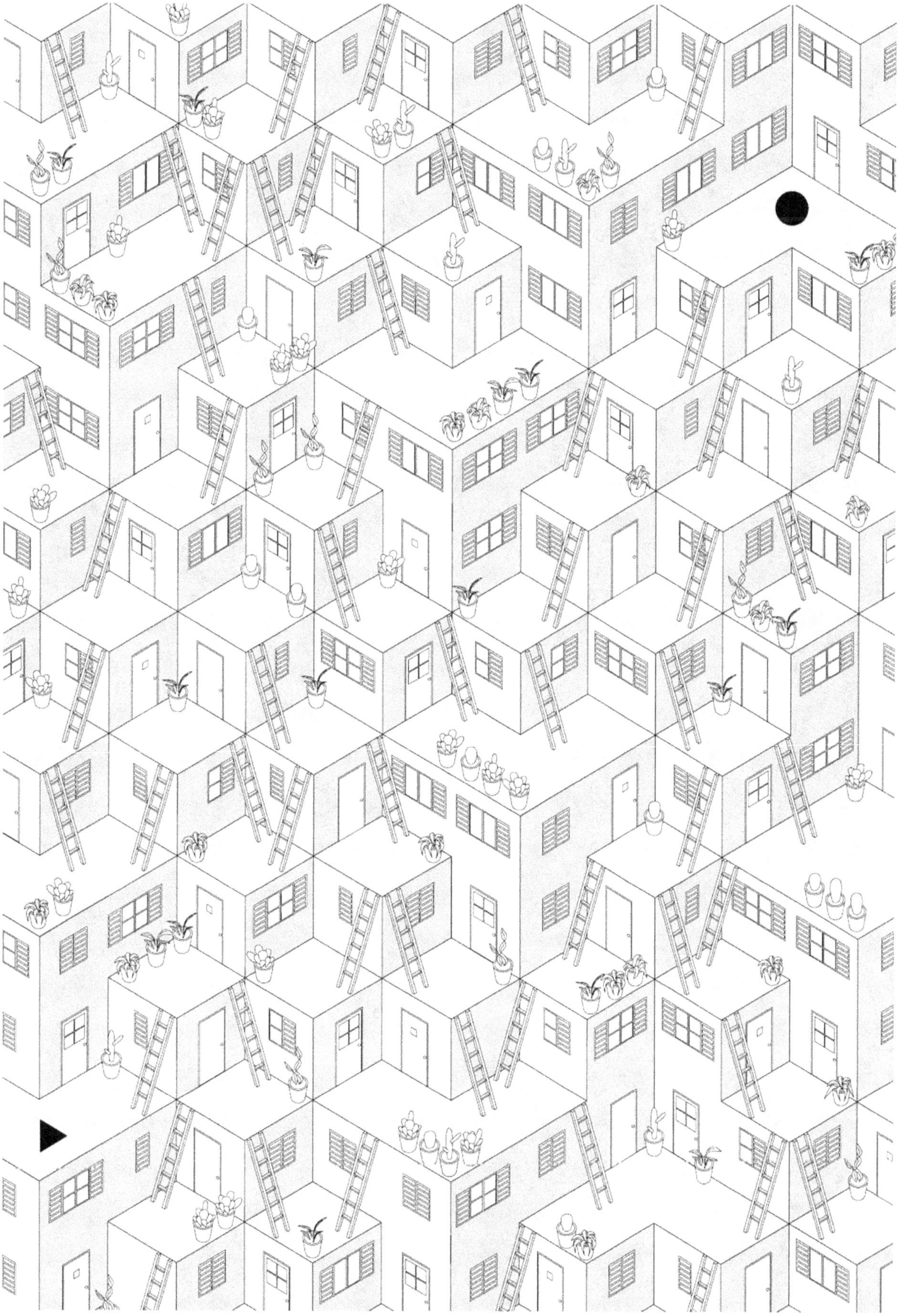

12

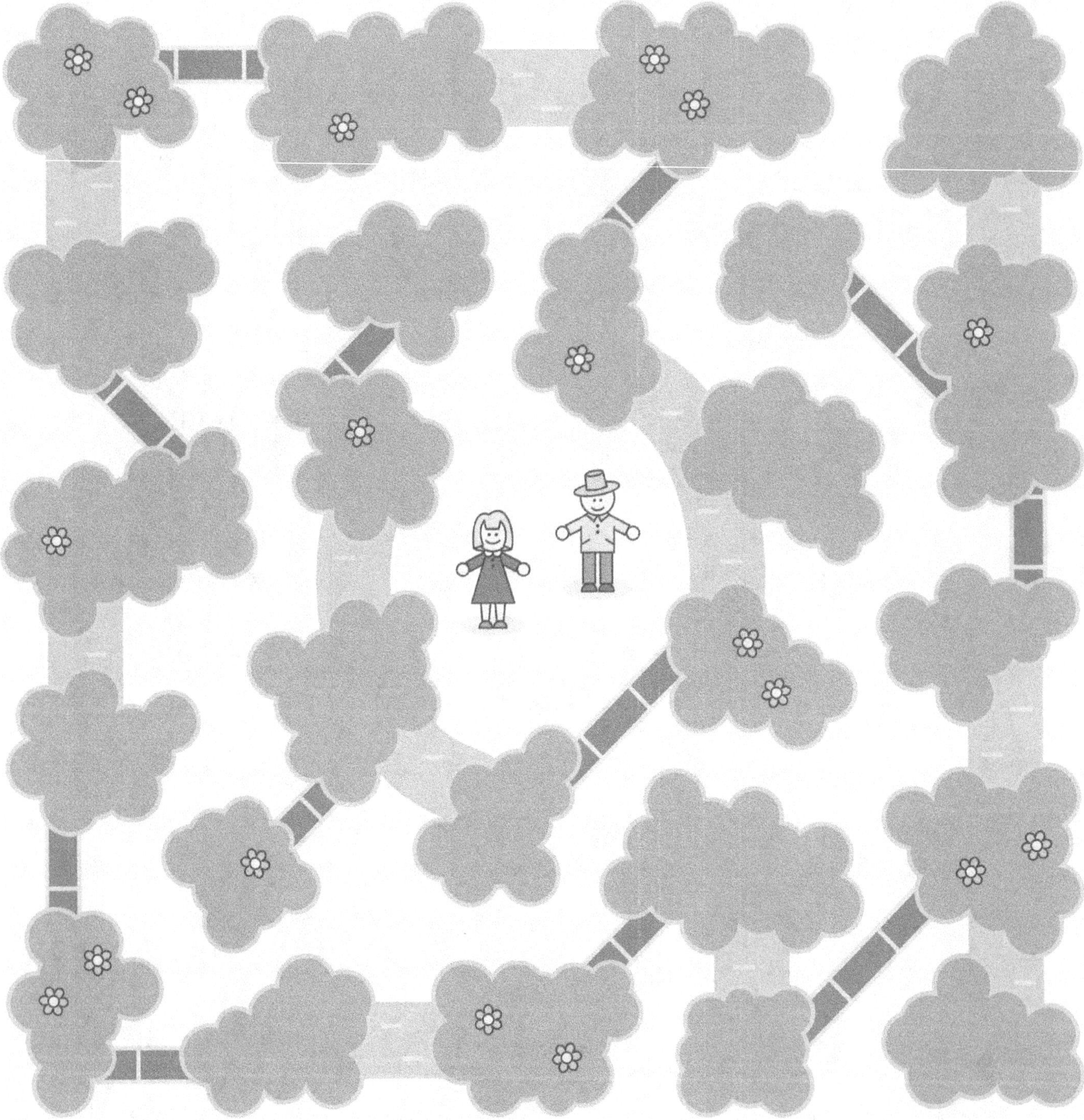

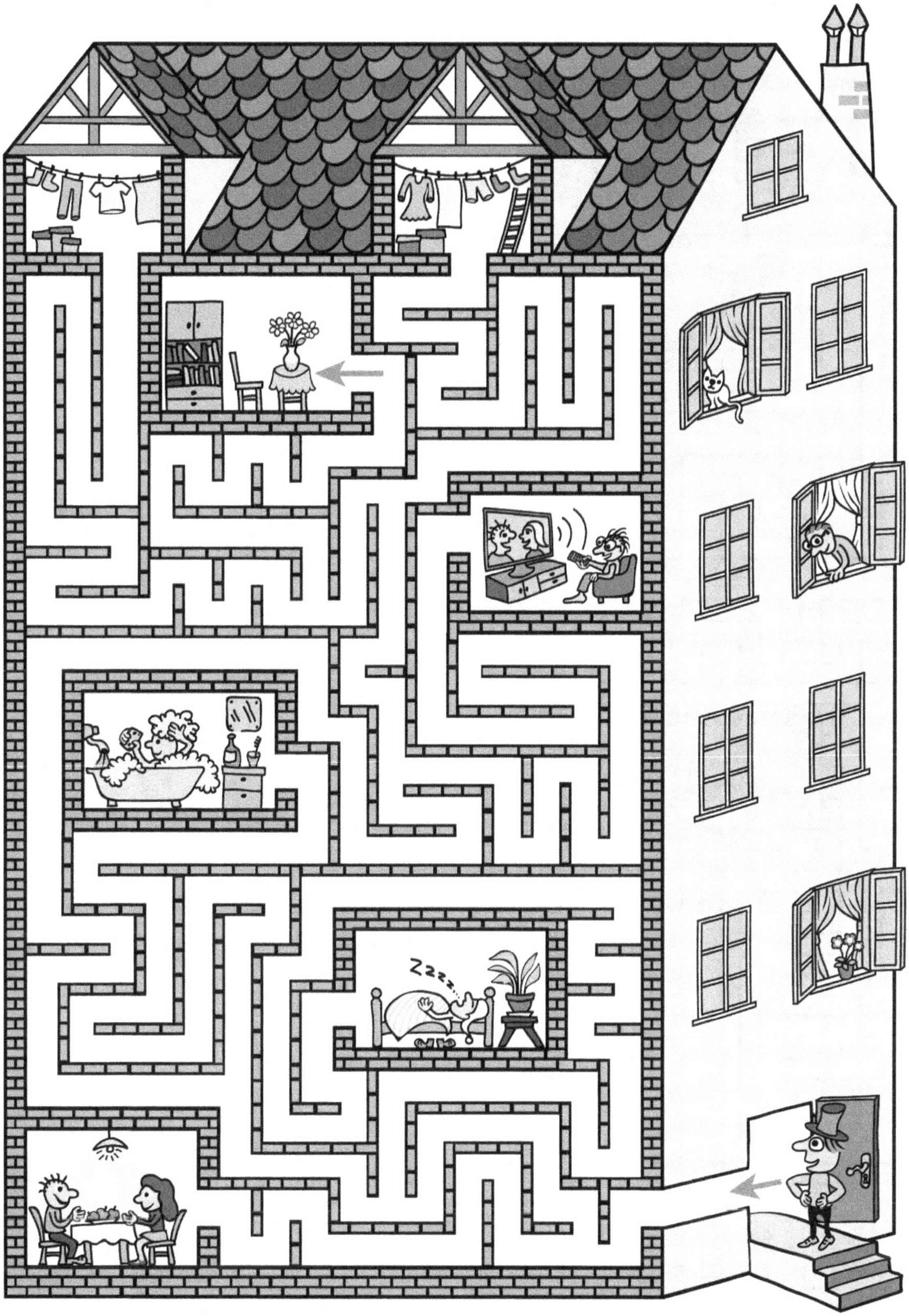

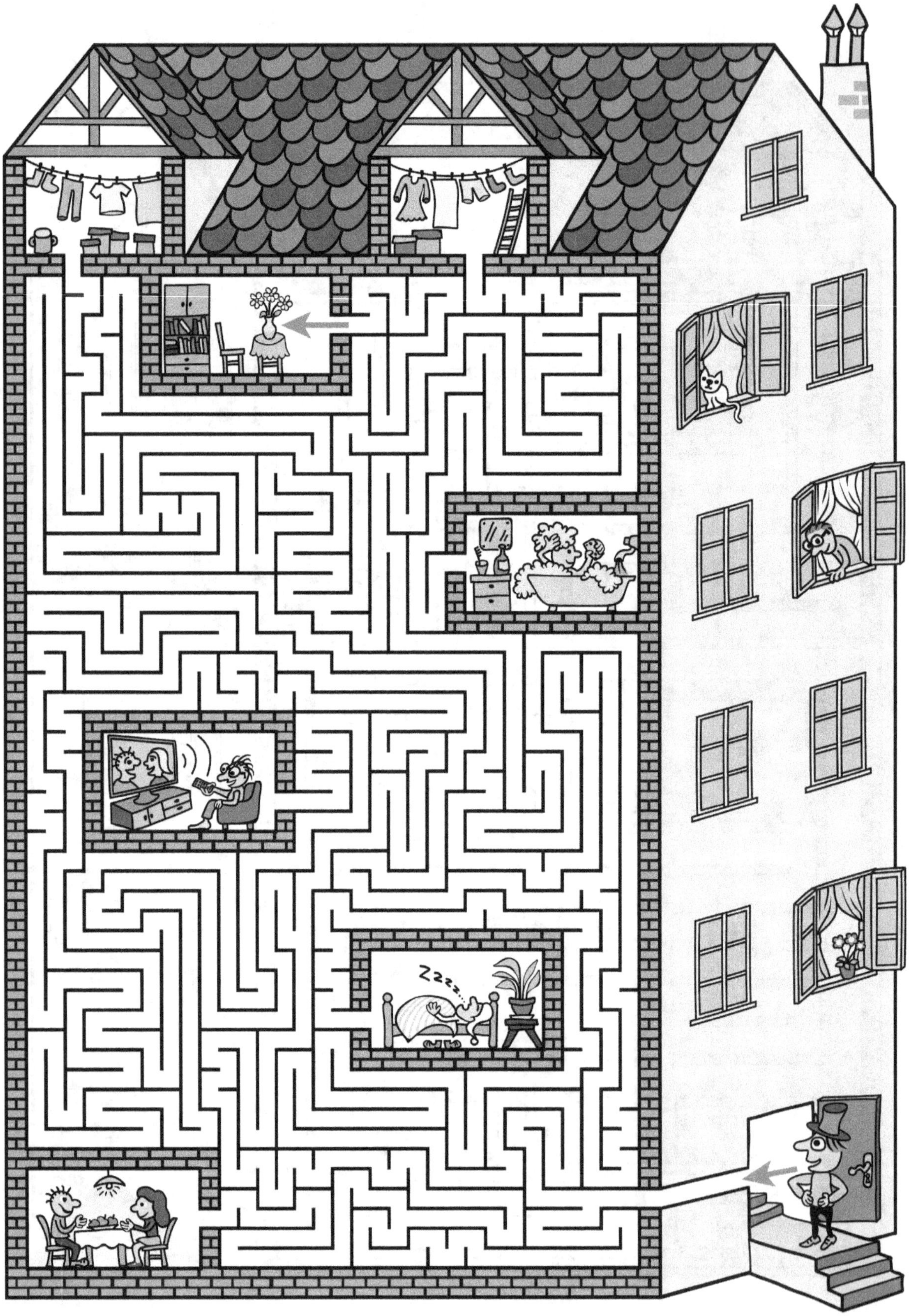

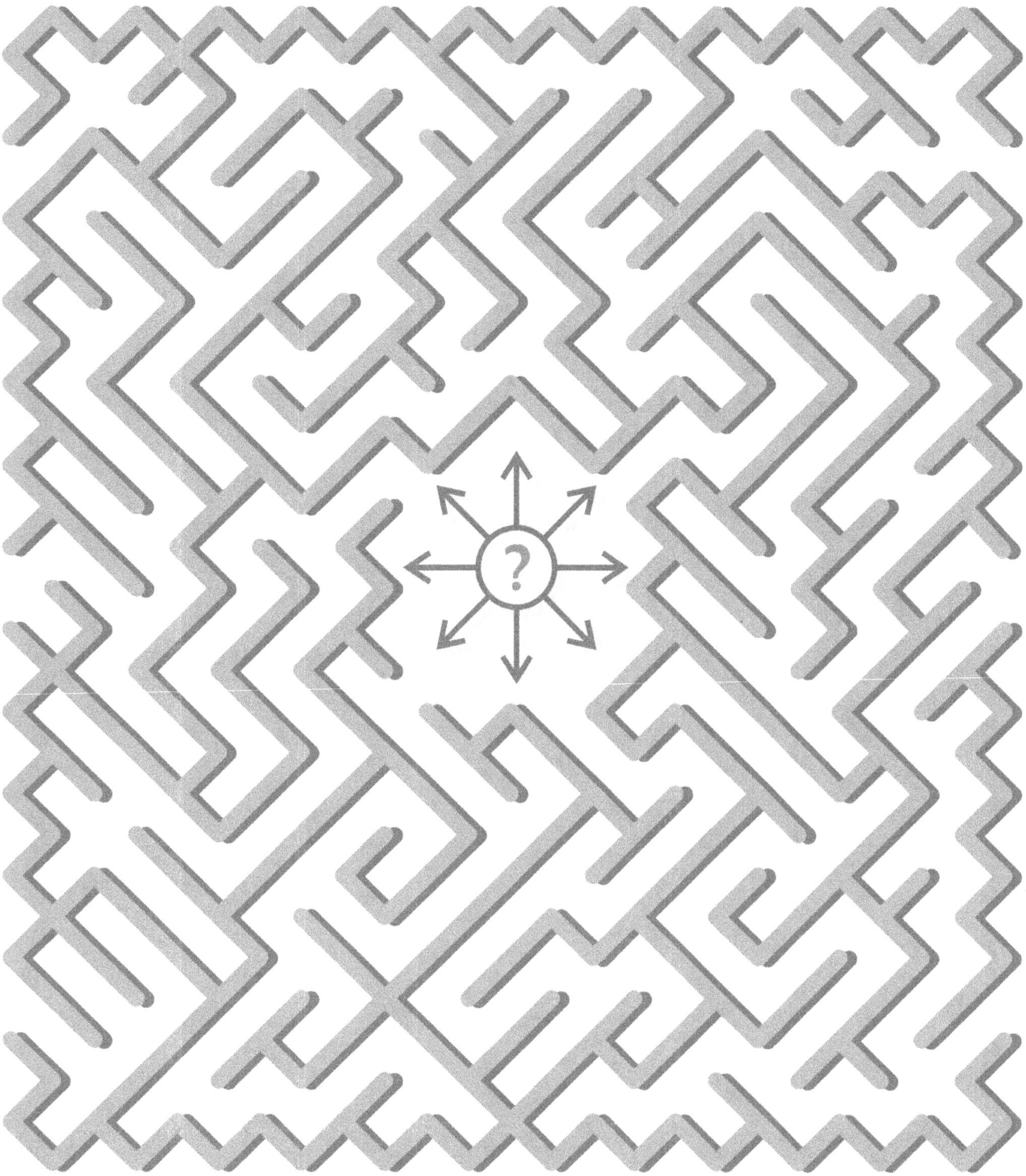

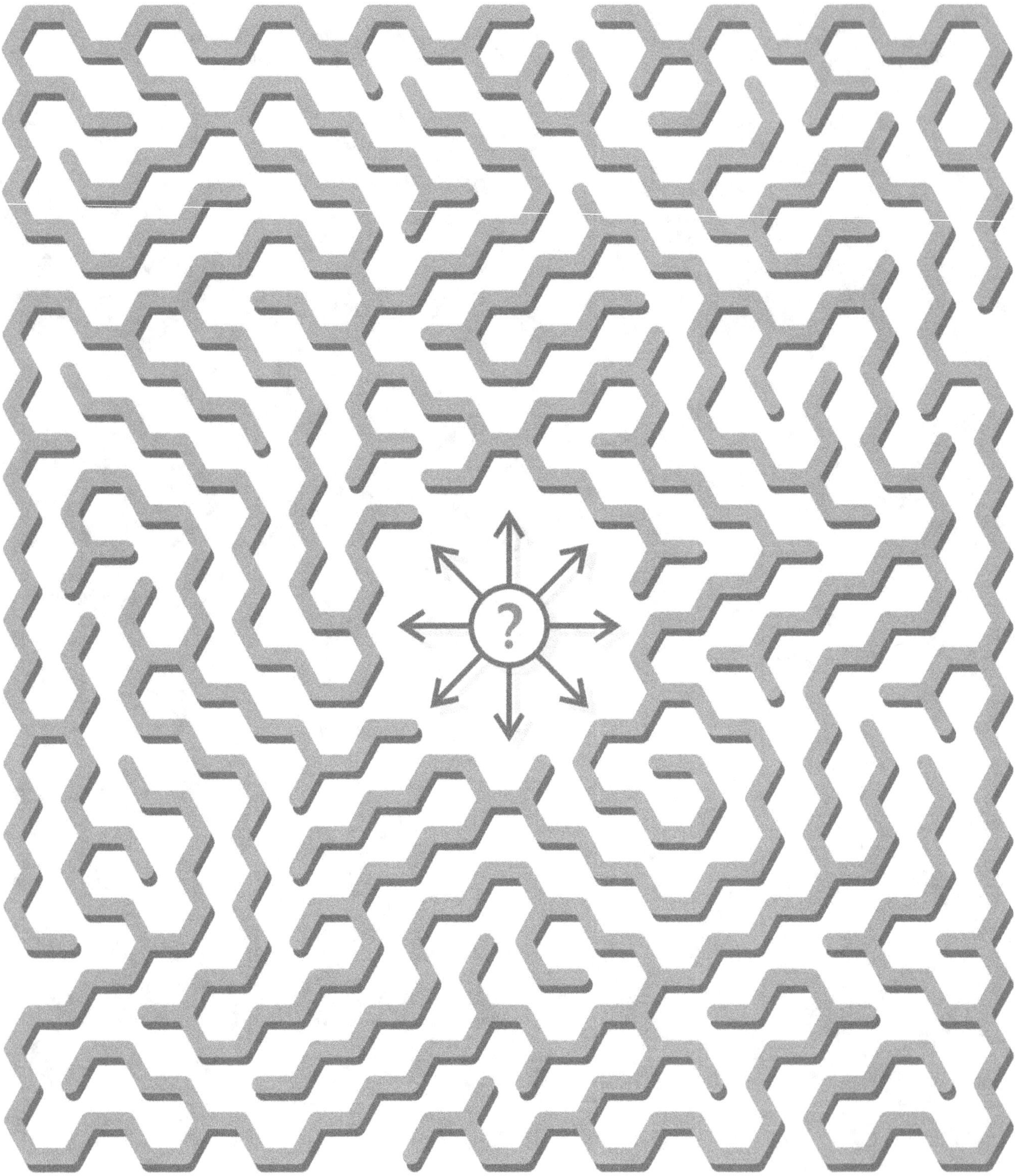

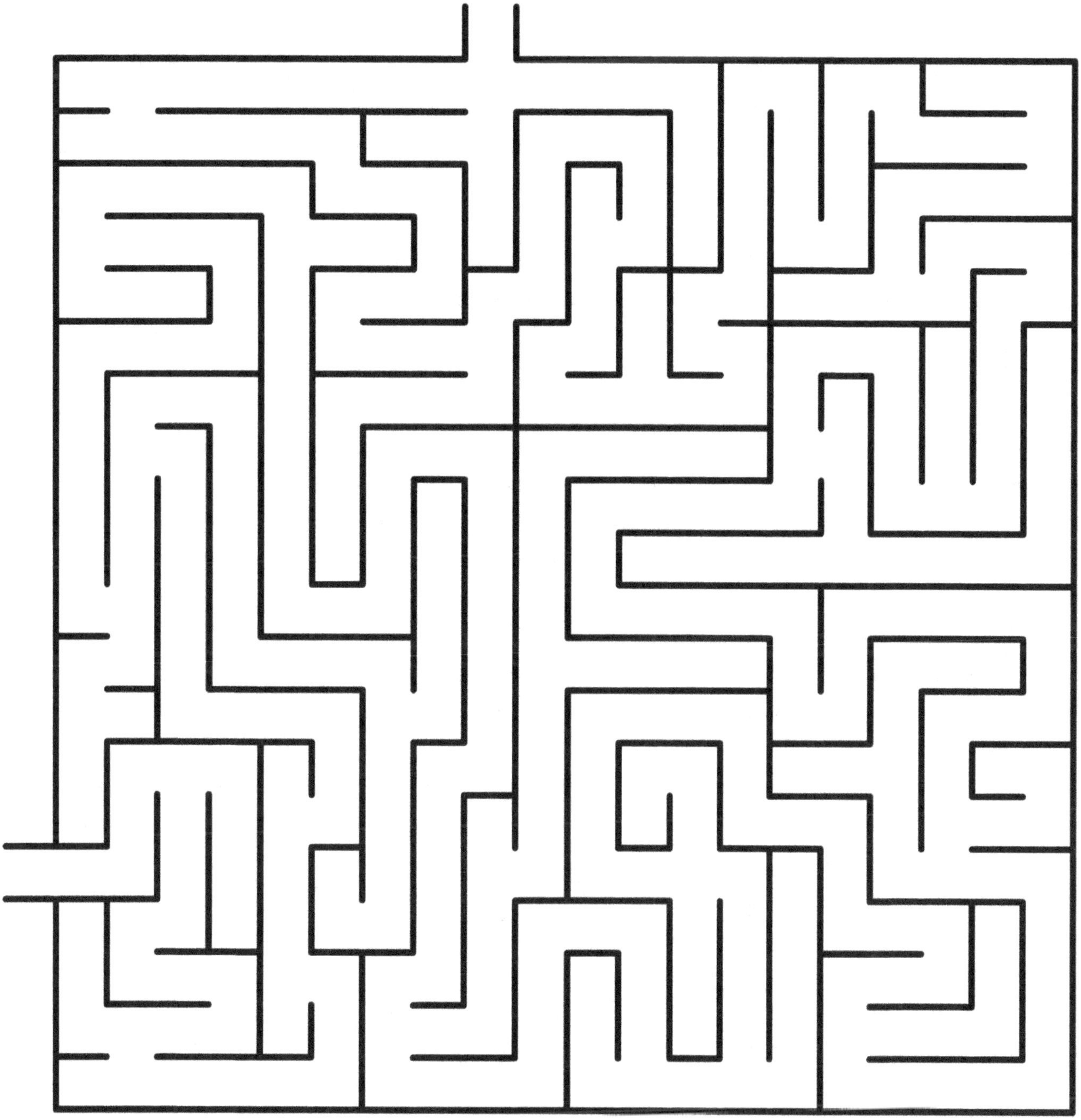

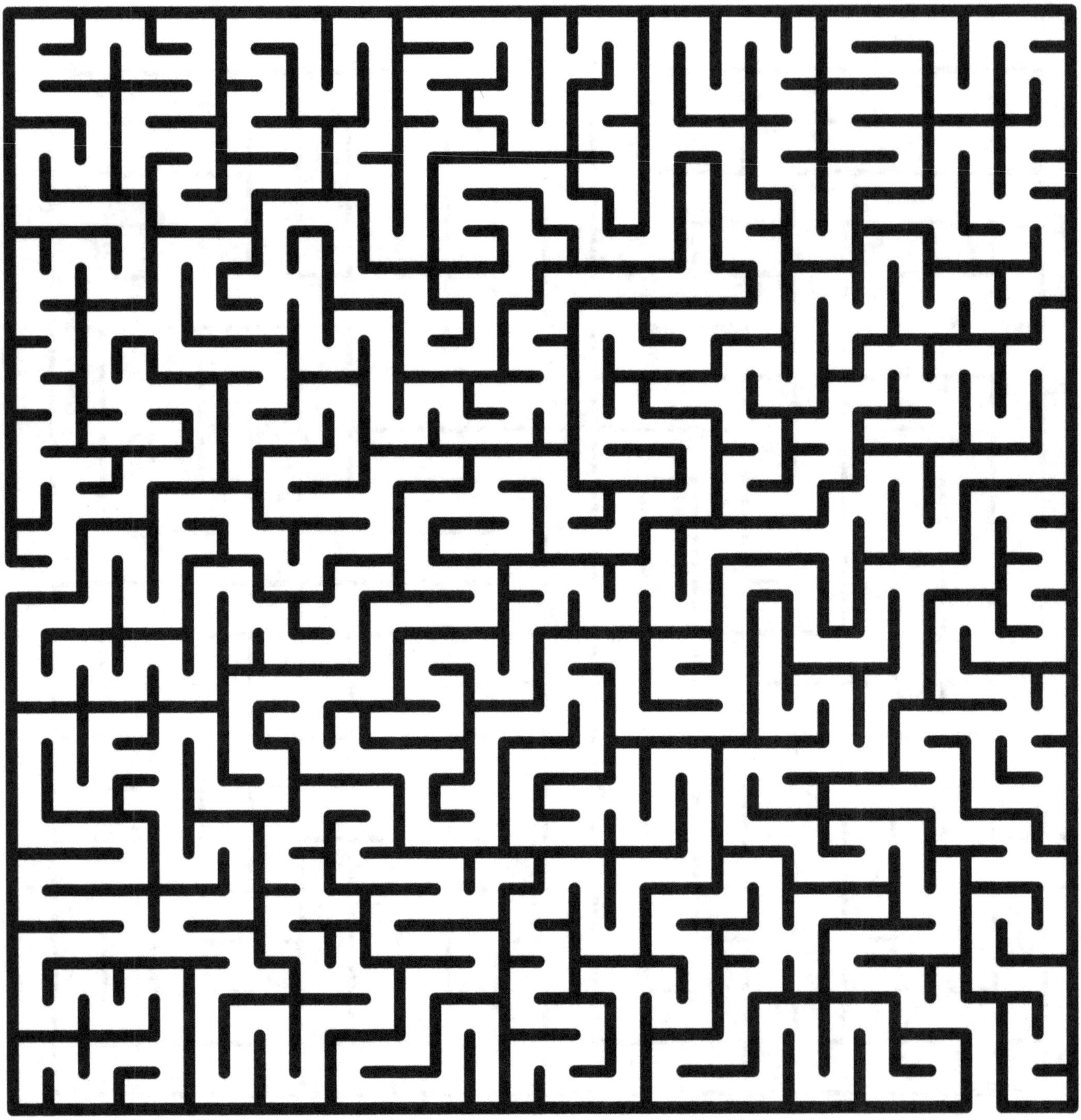

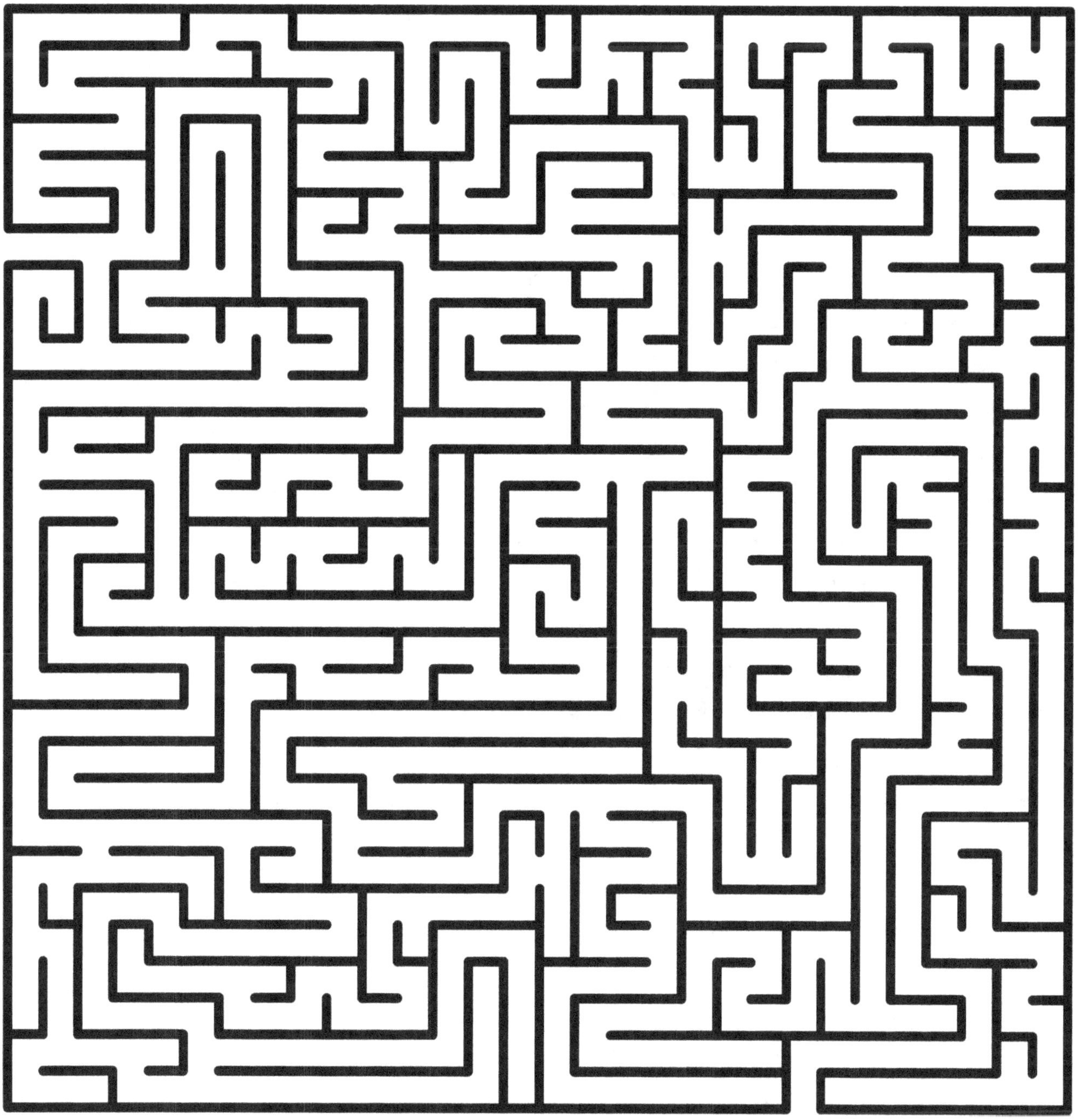

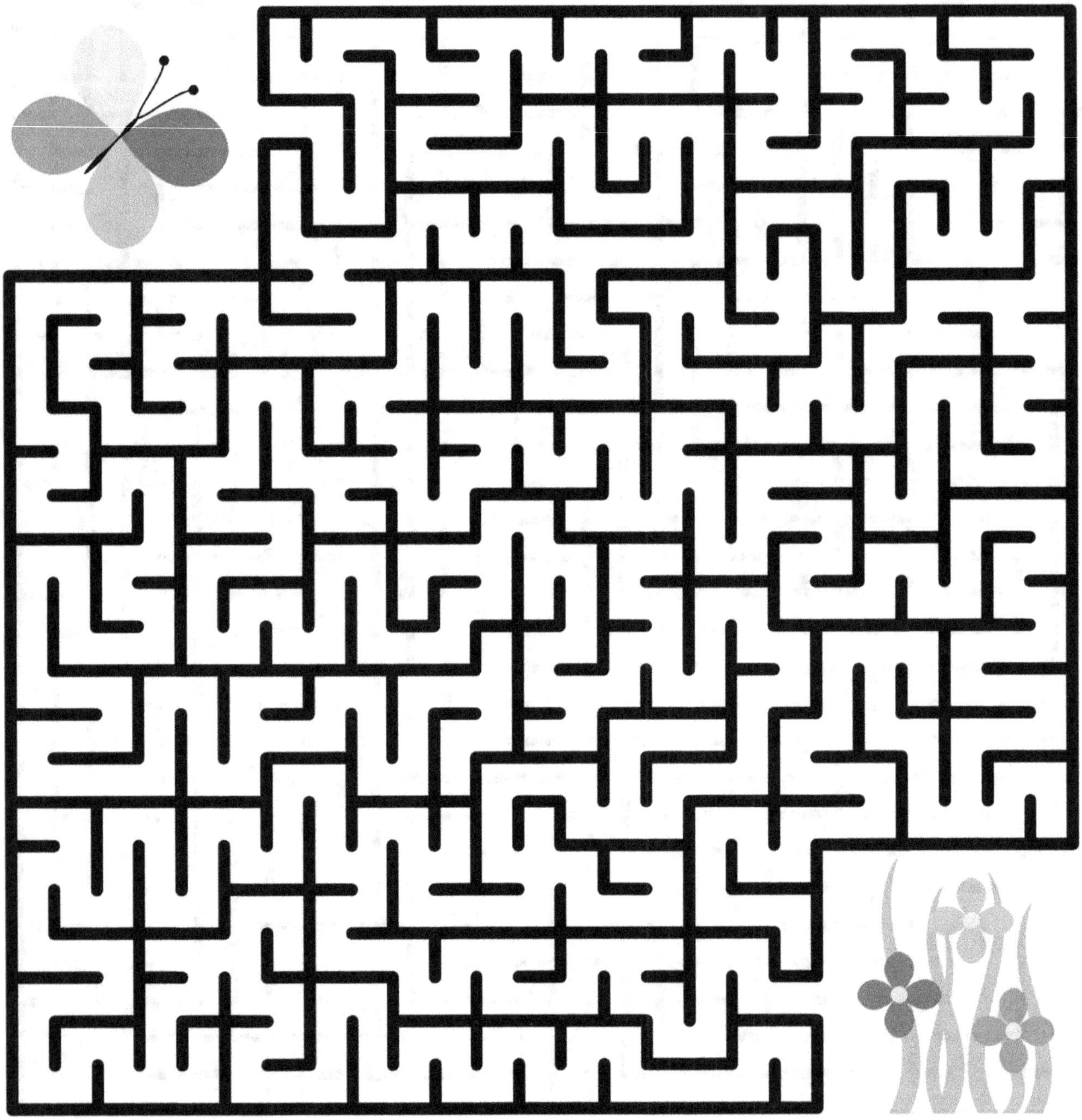

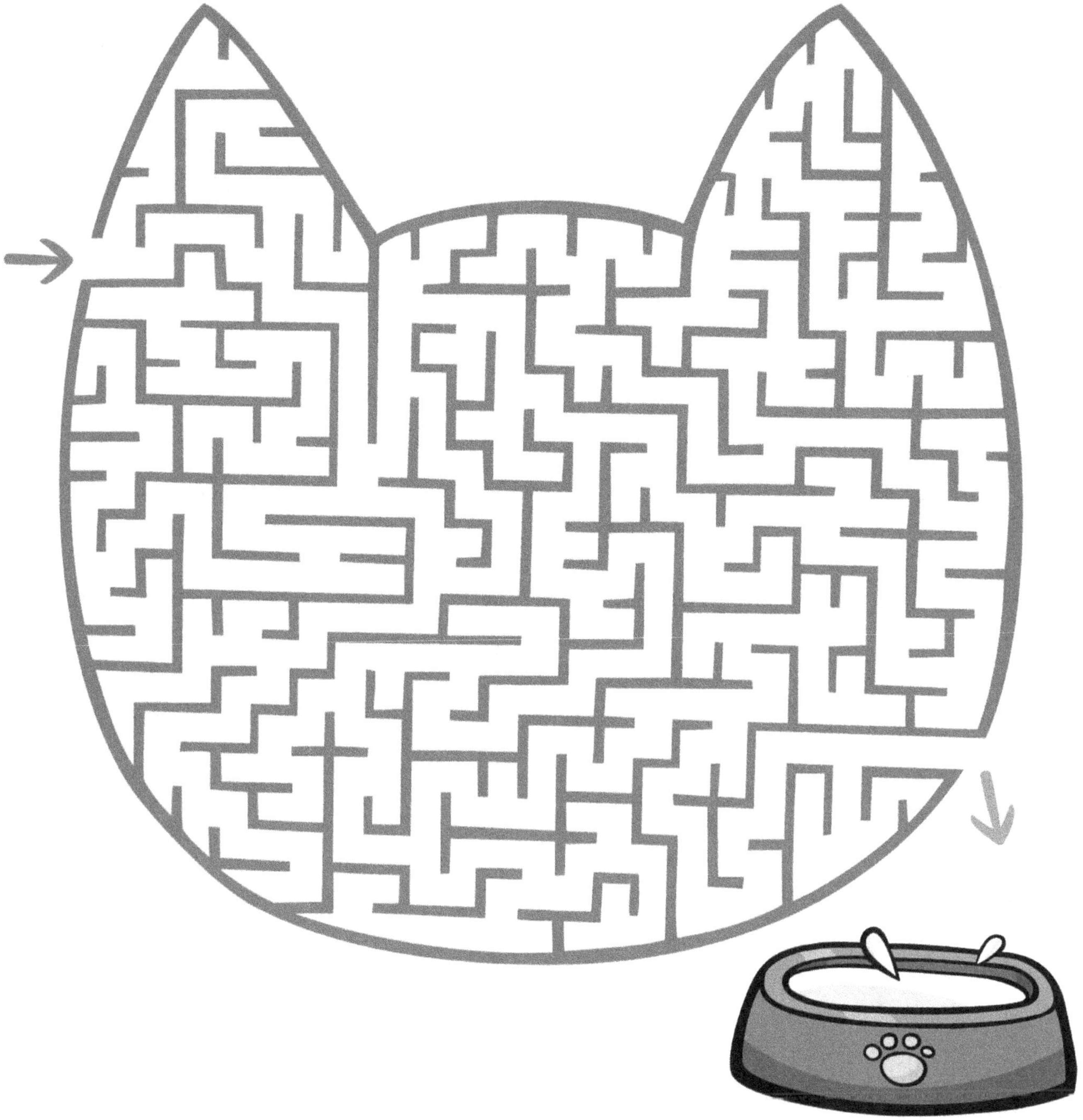

19

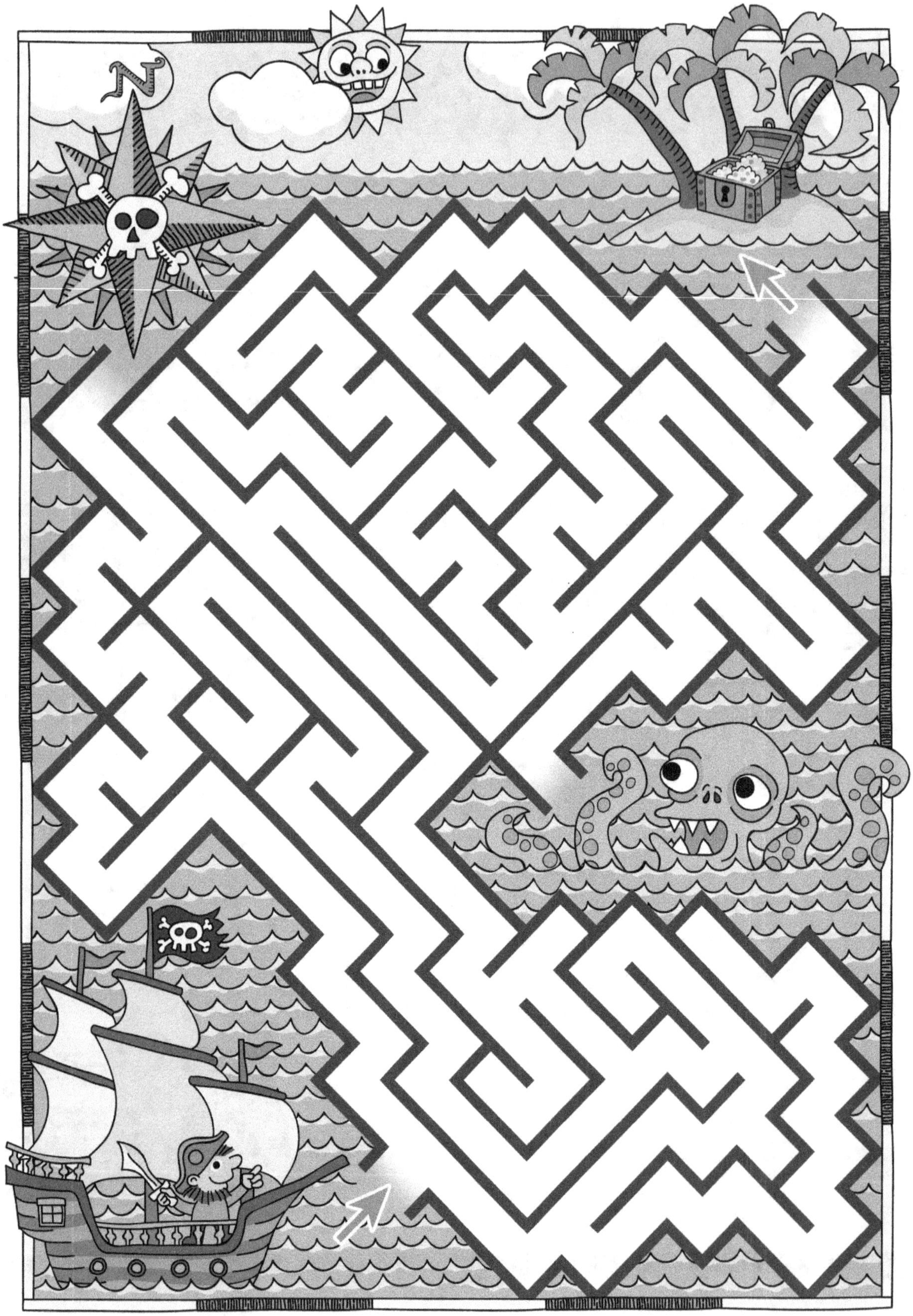

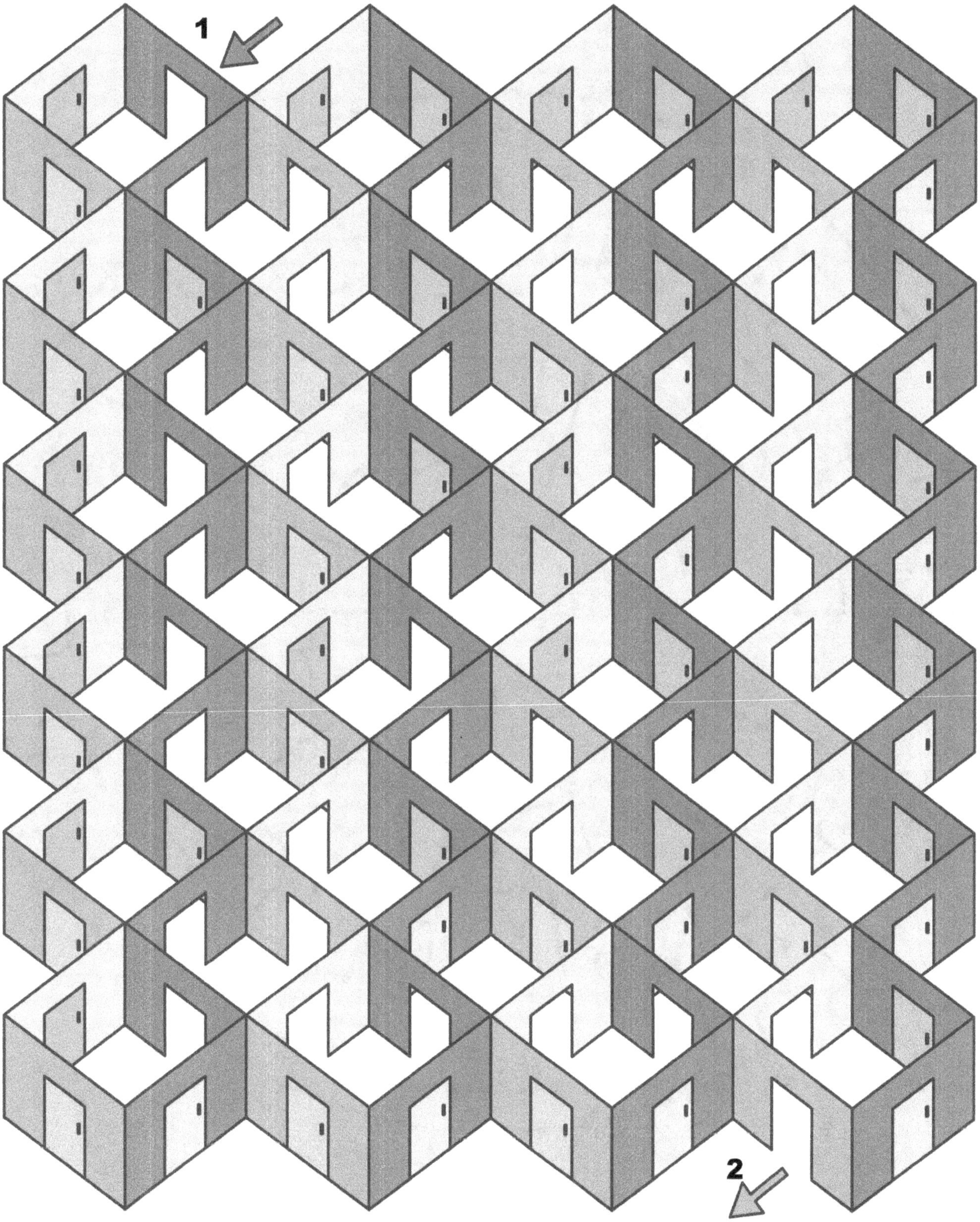

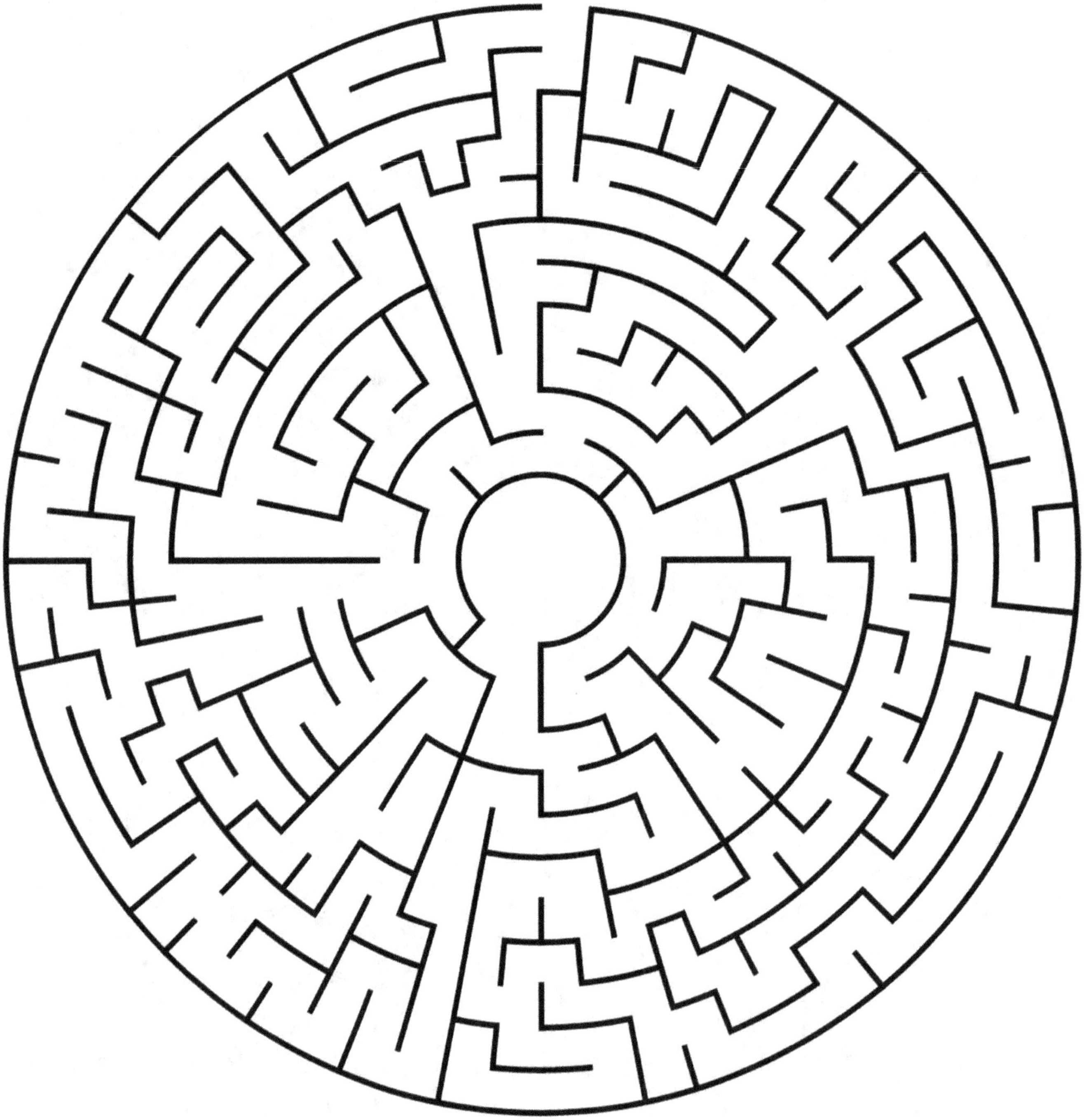

23

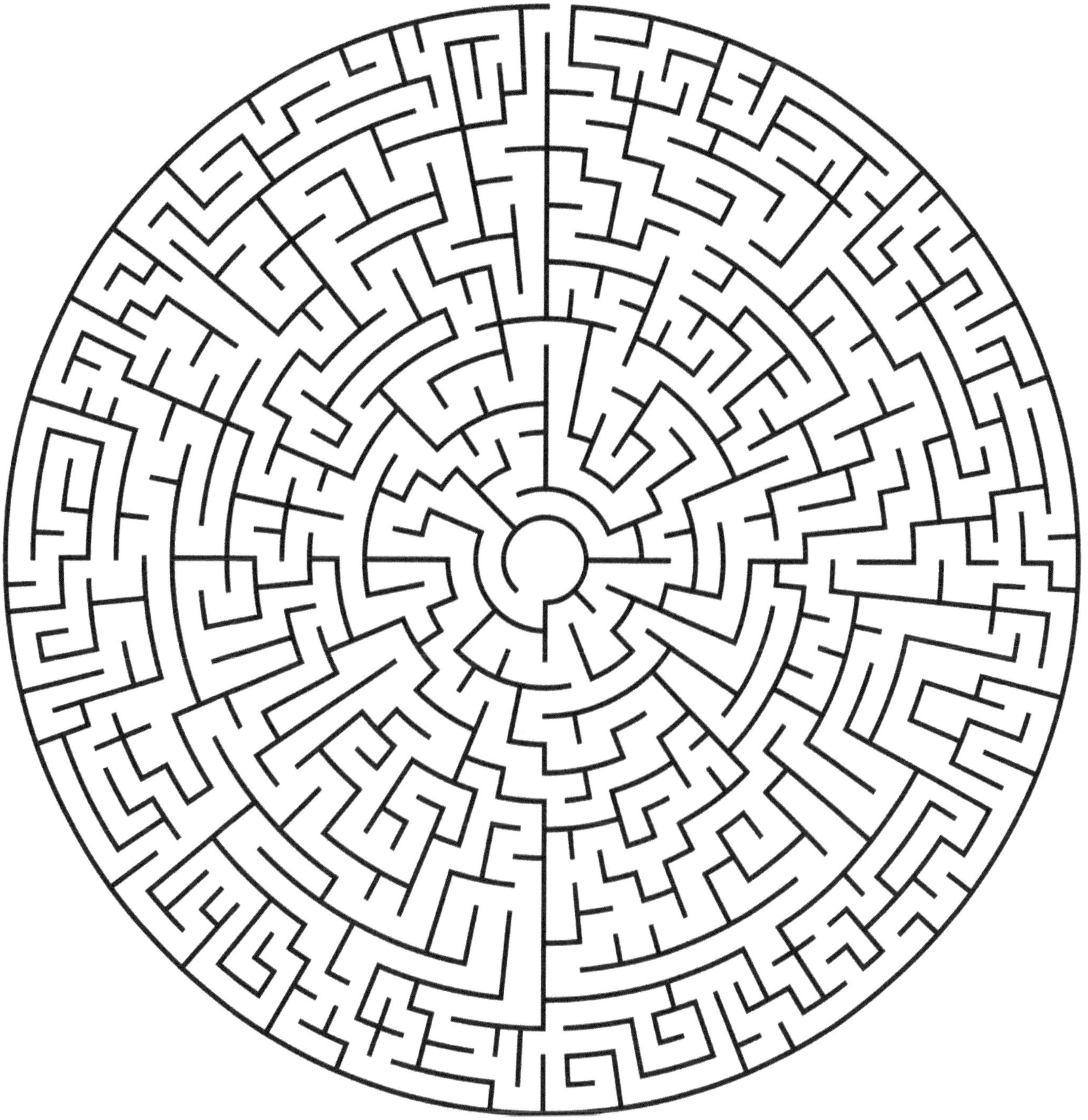

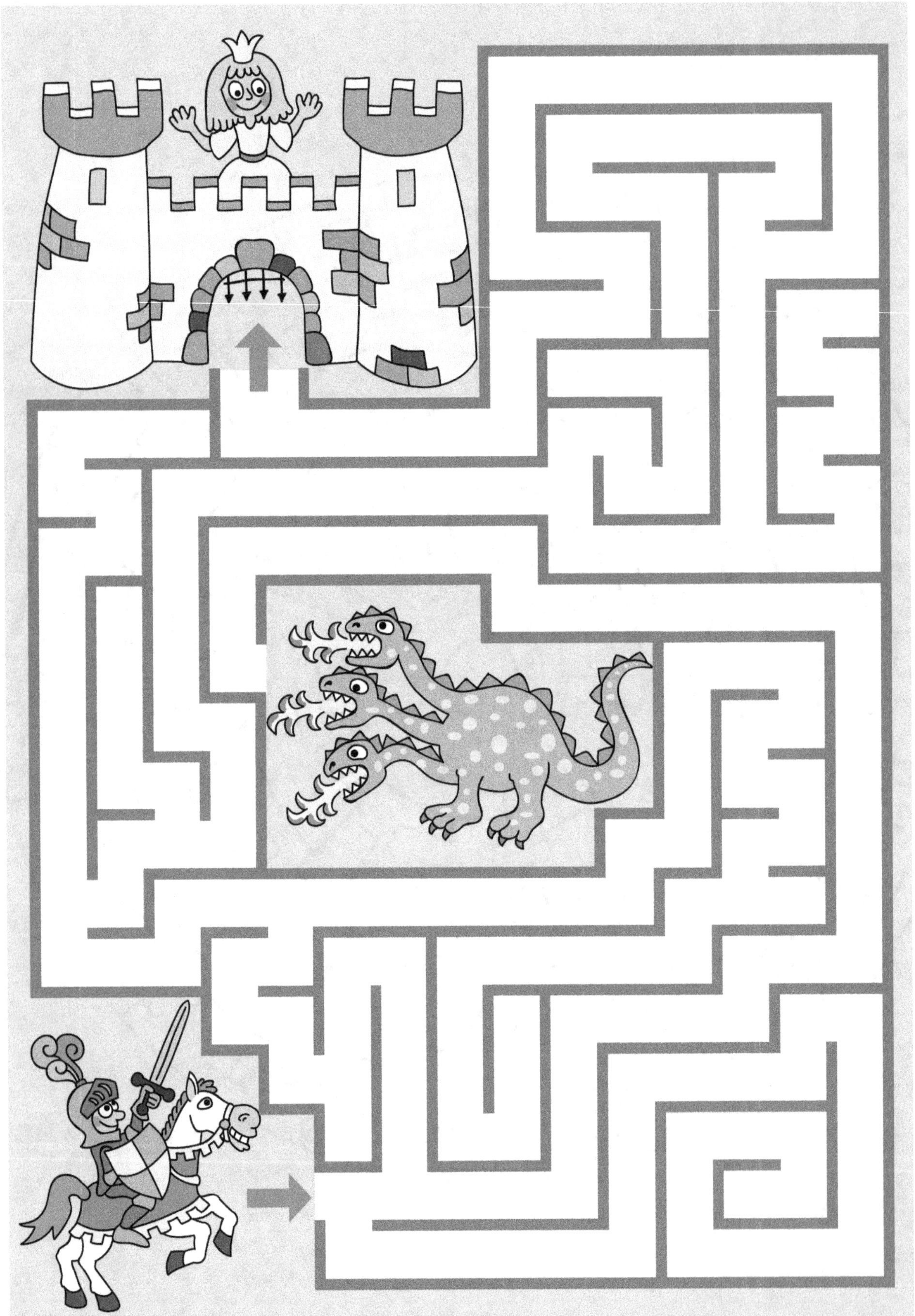

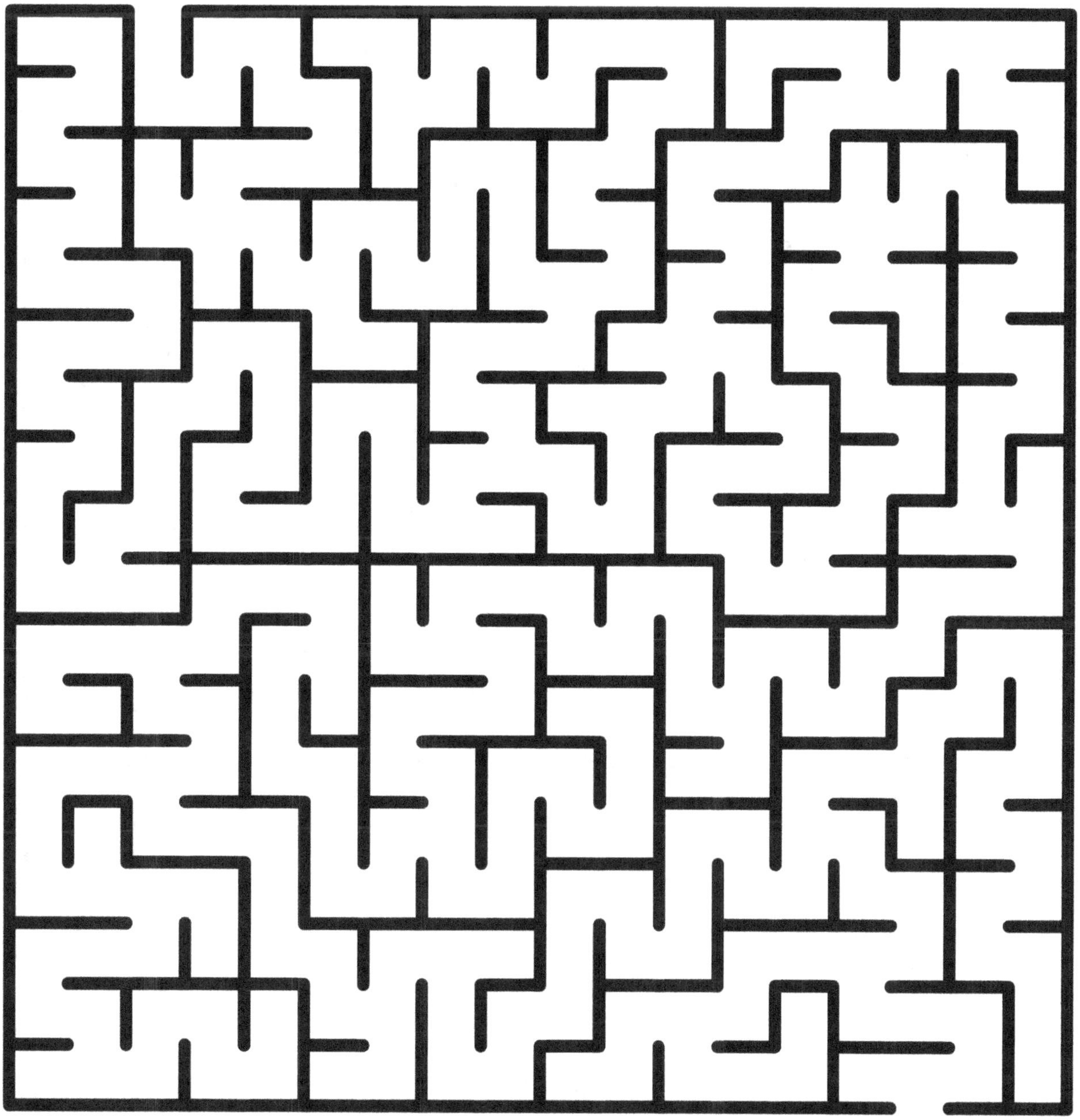

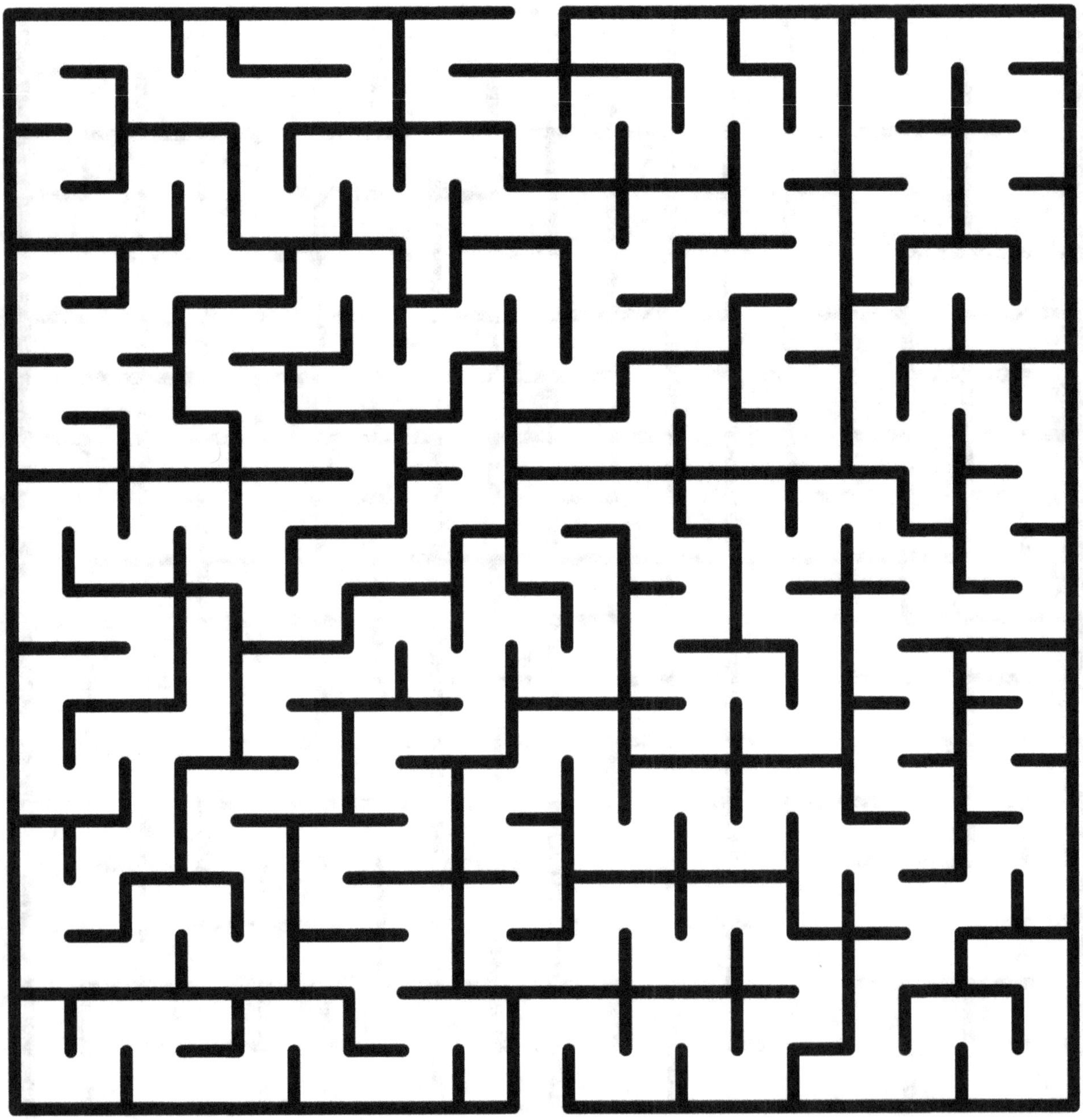

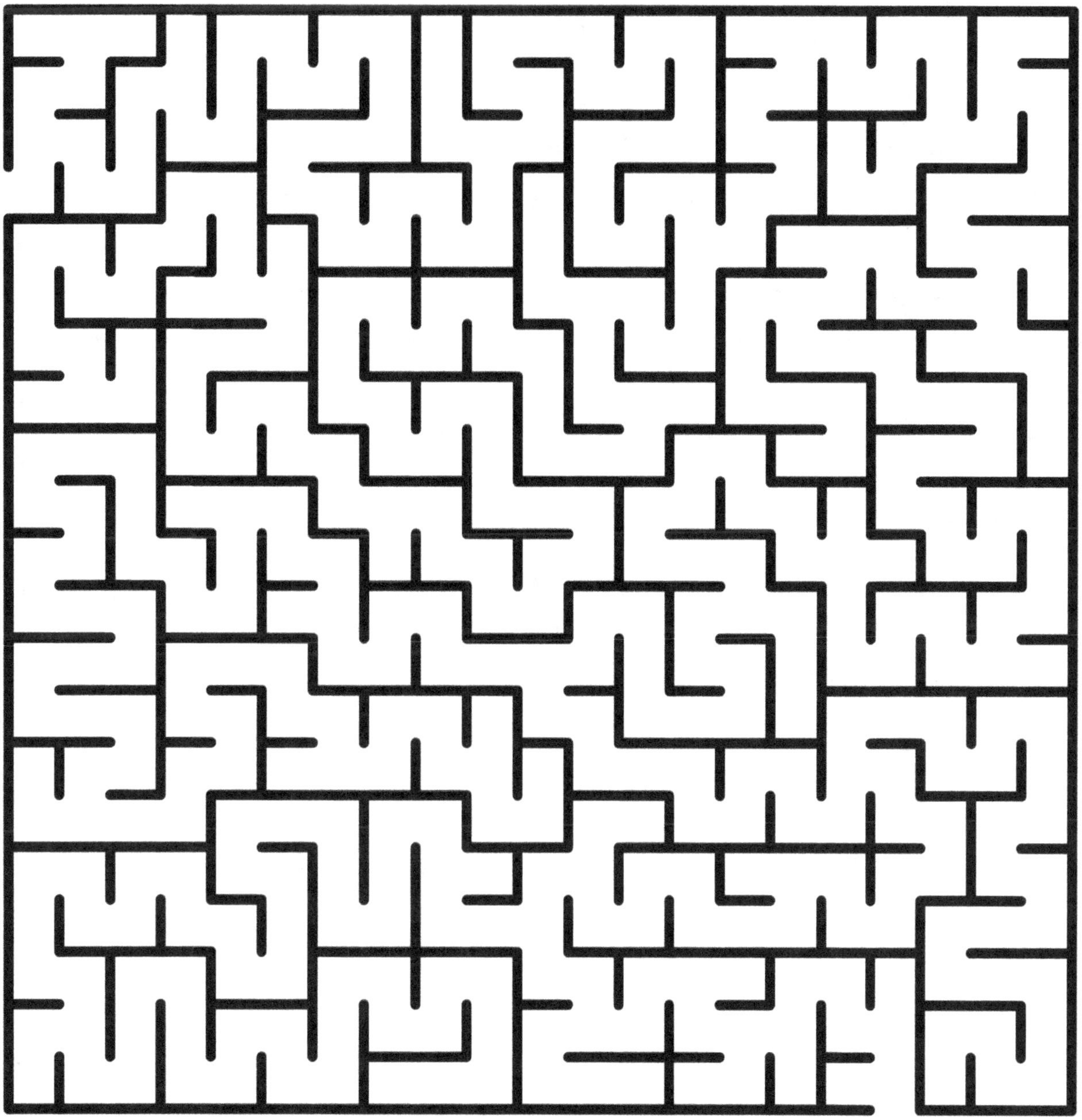

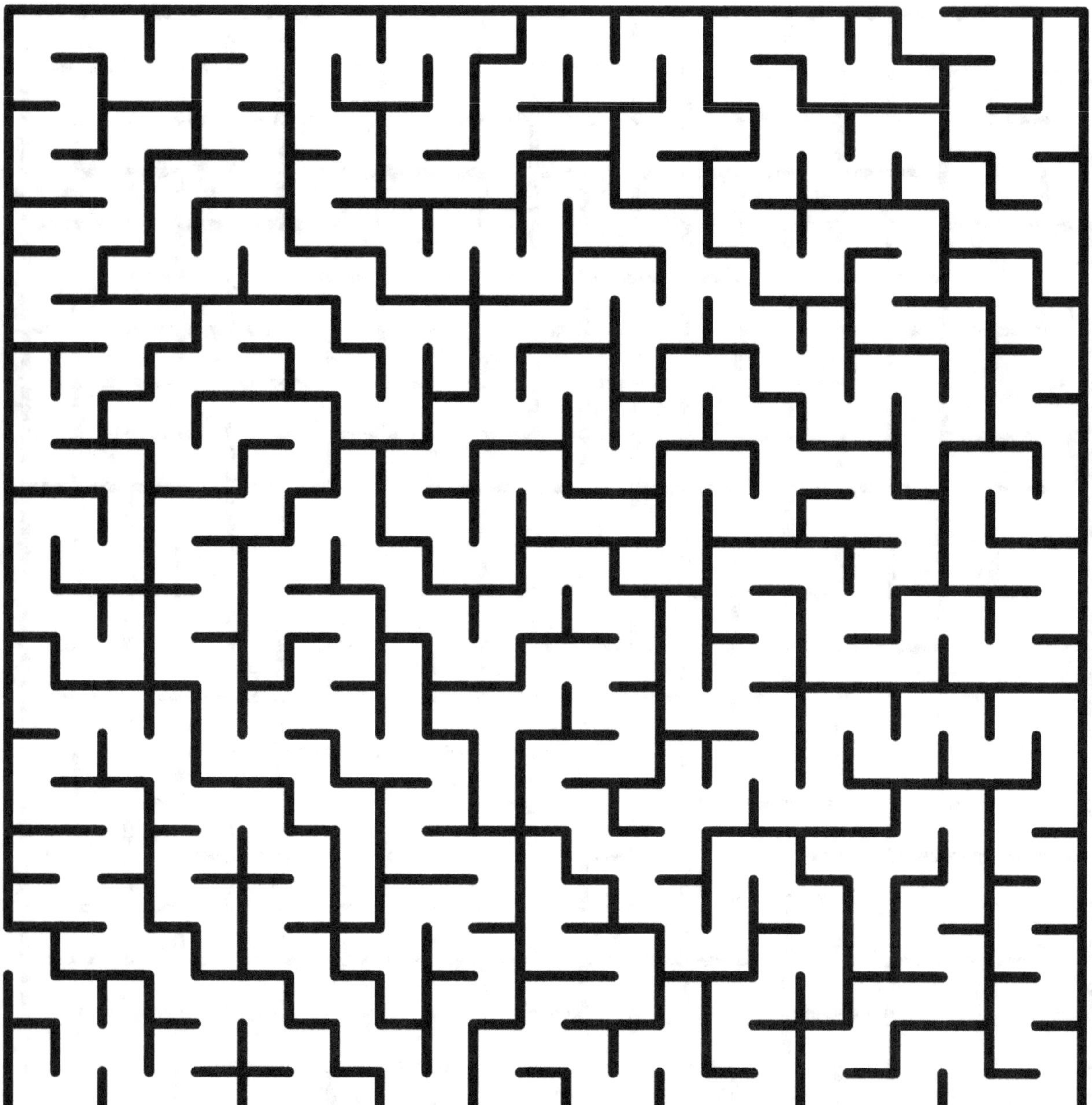

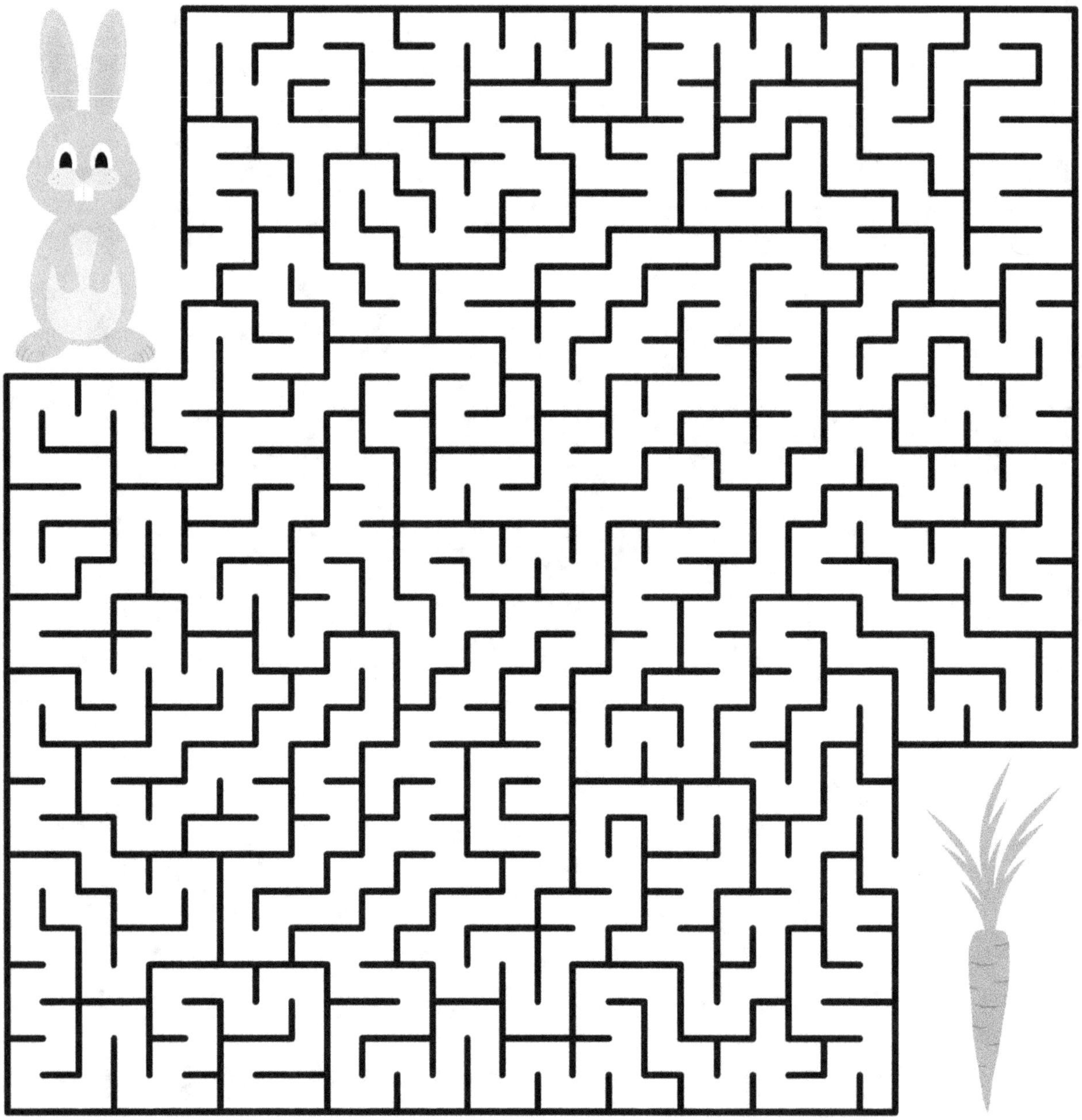

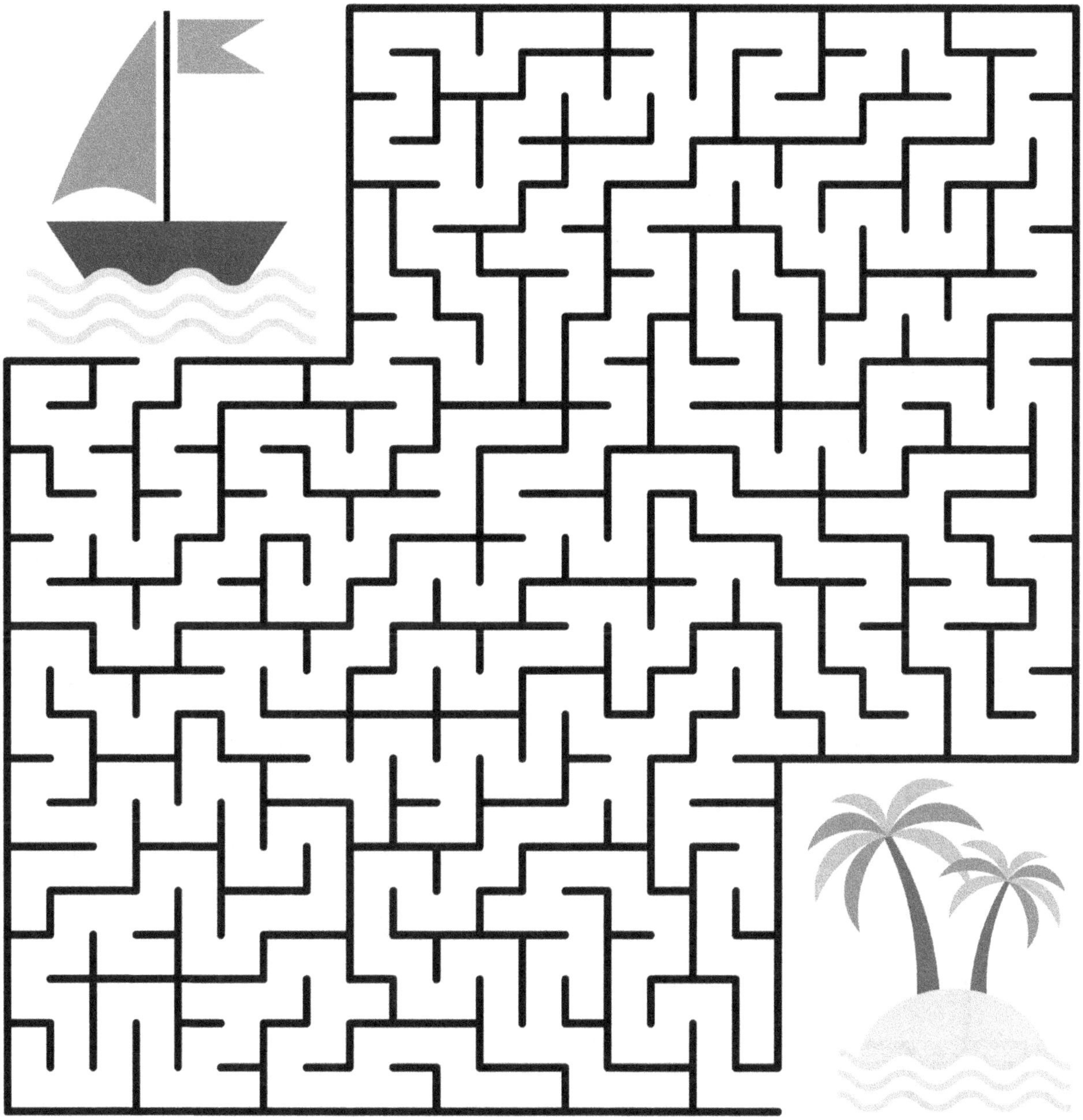

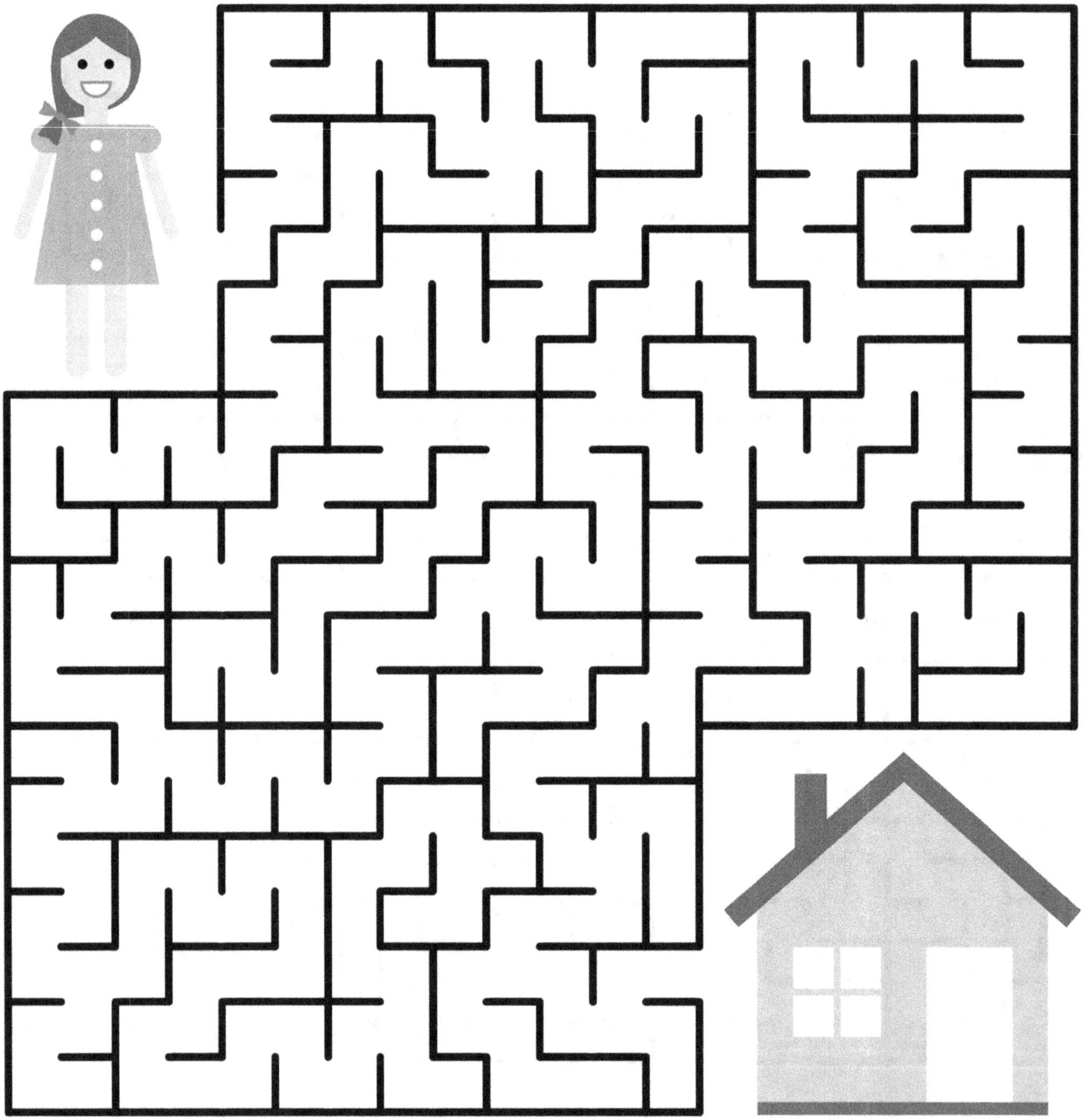

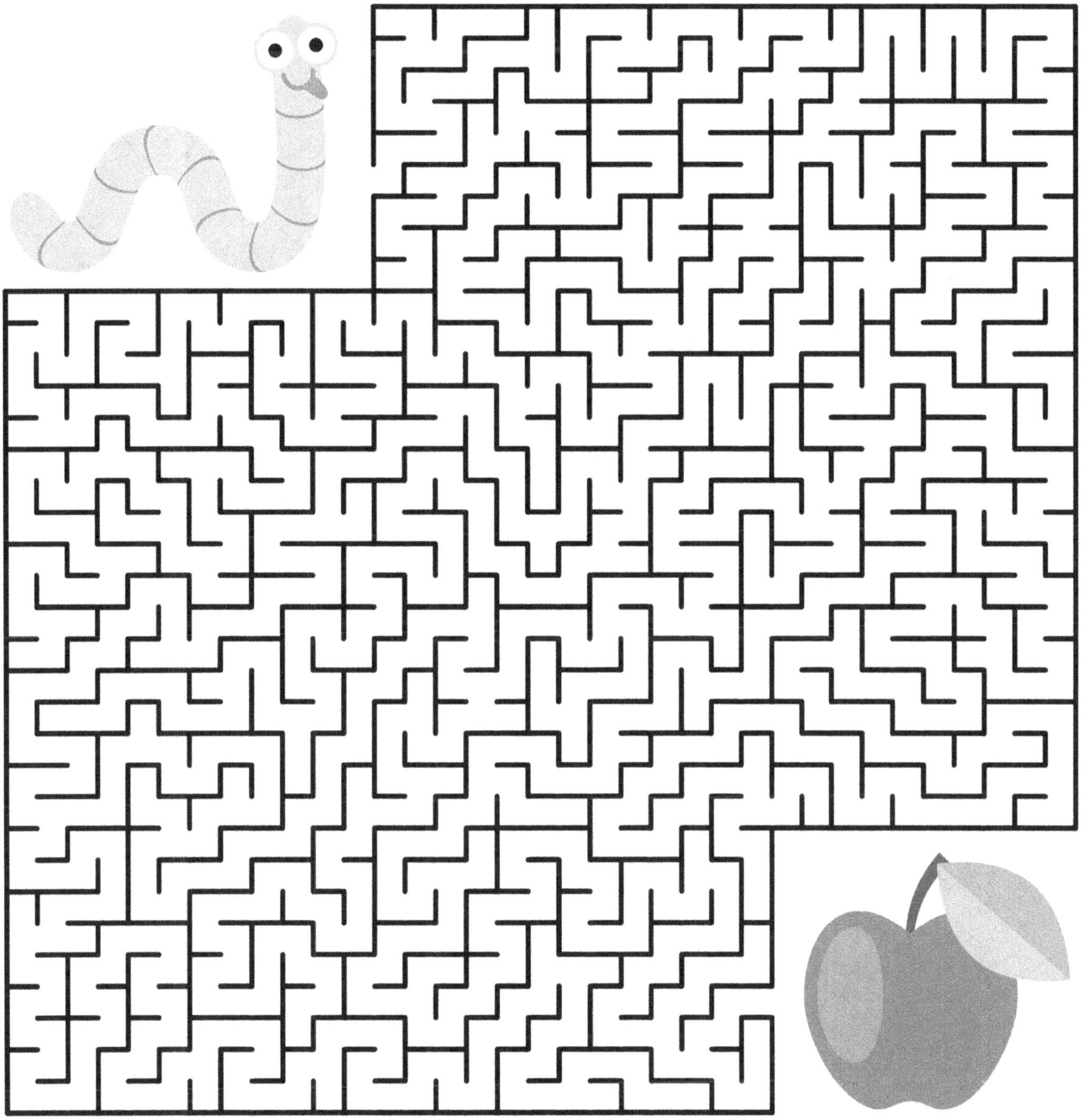

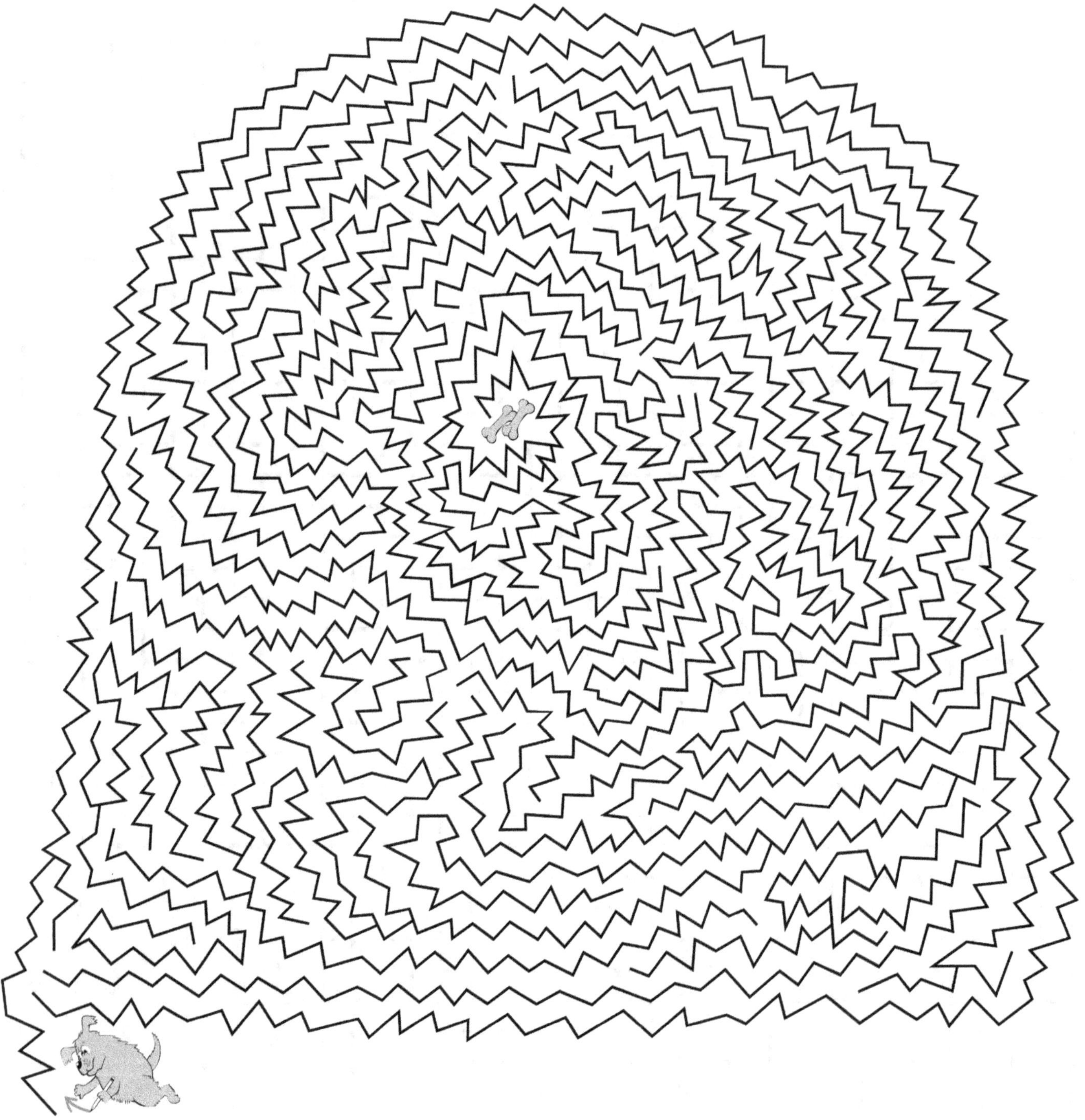

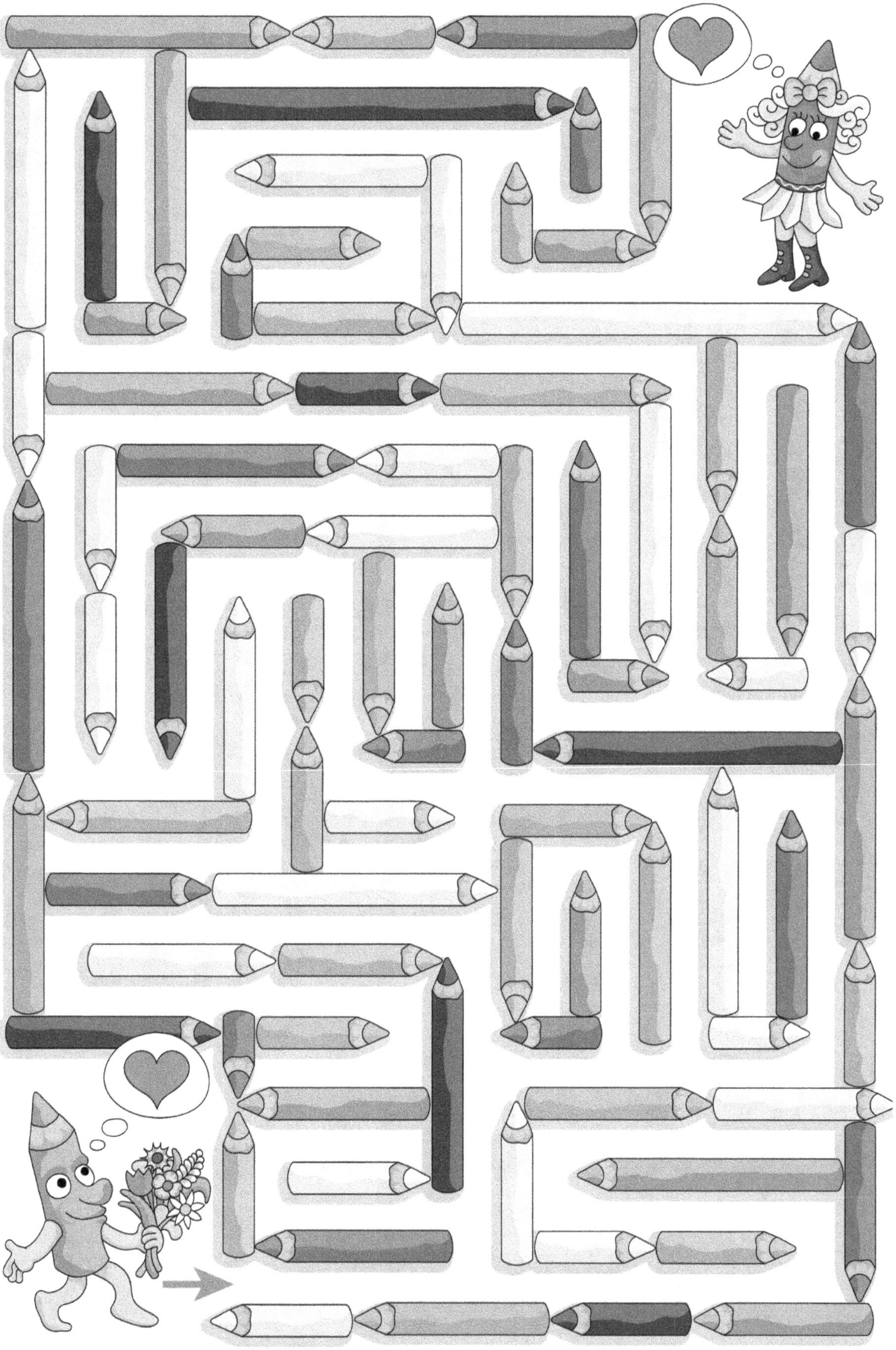

36

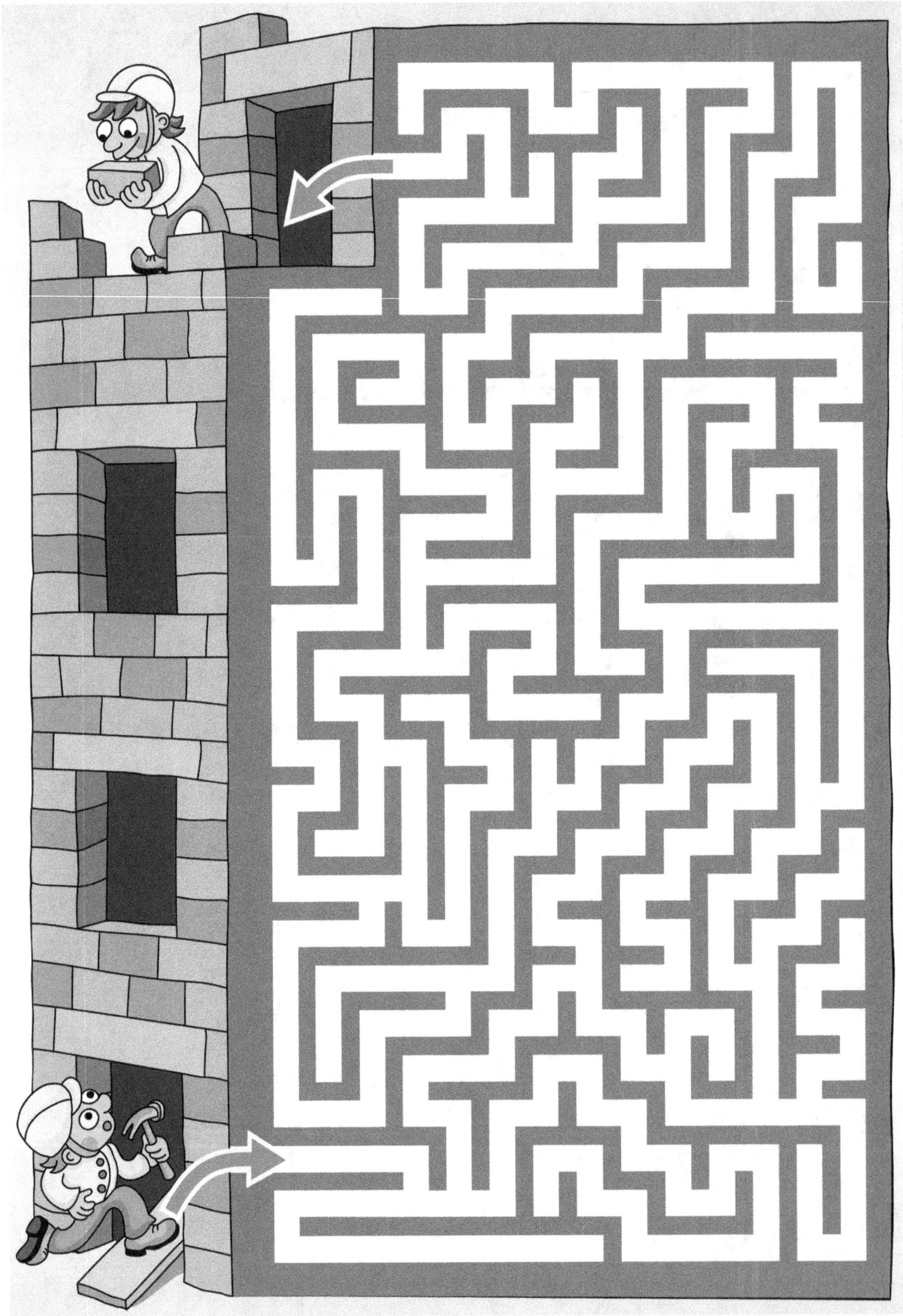

37

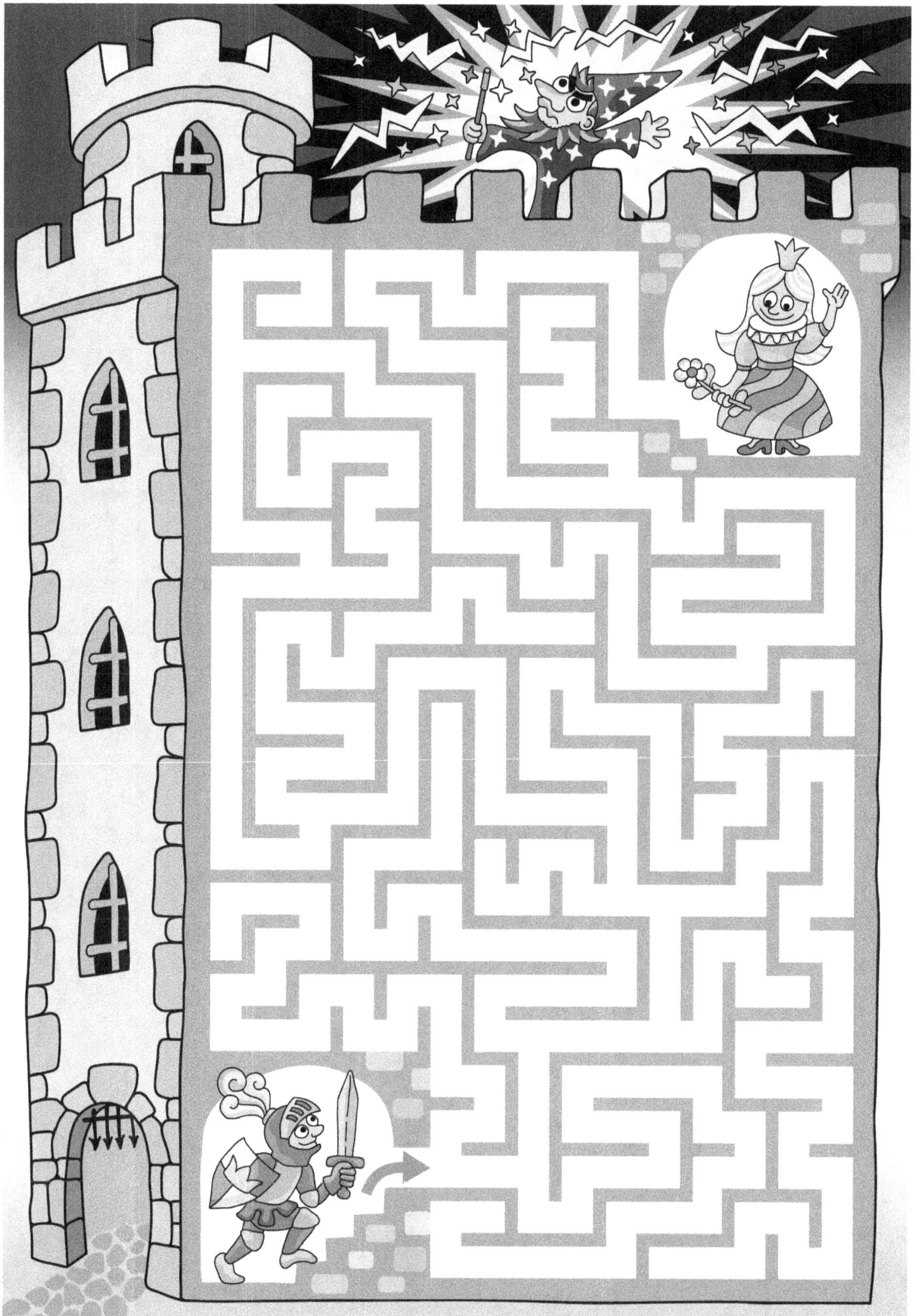

HOSPITAL

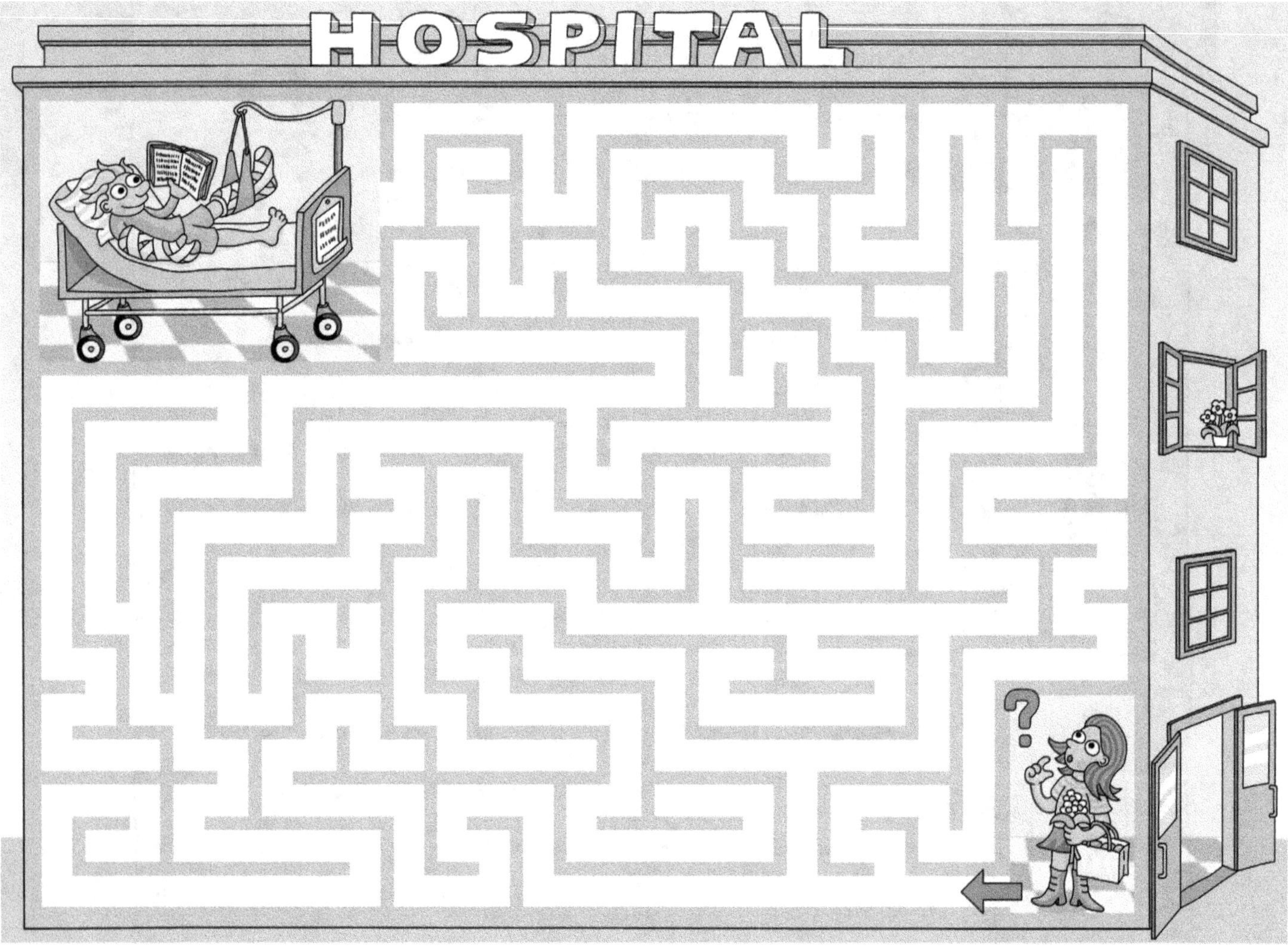

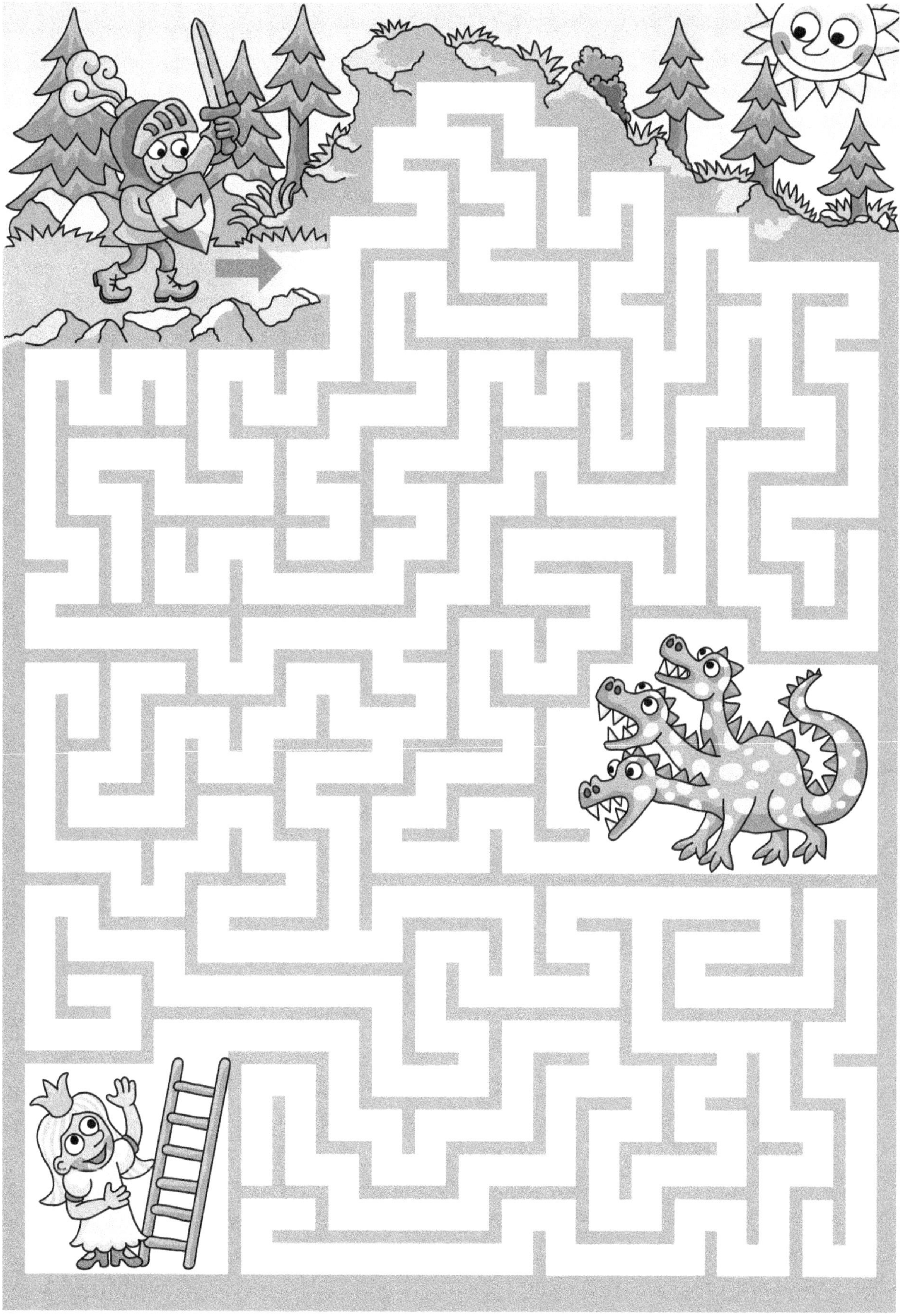

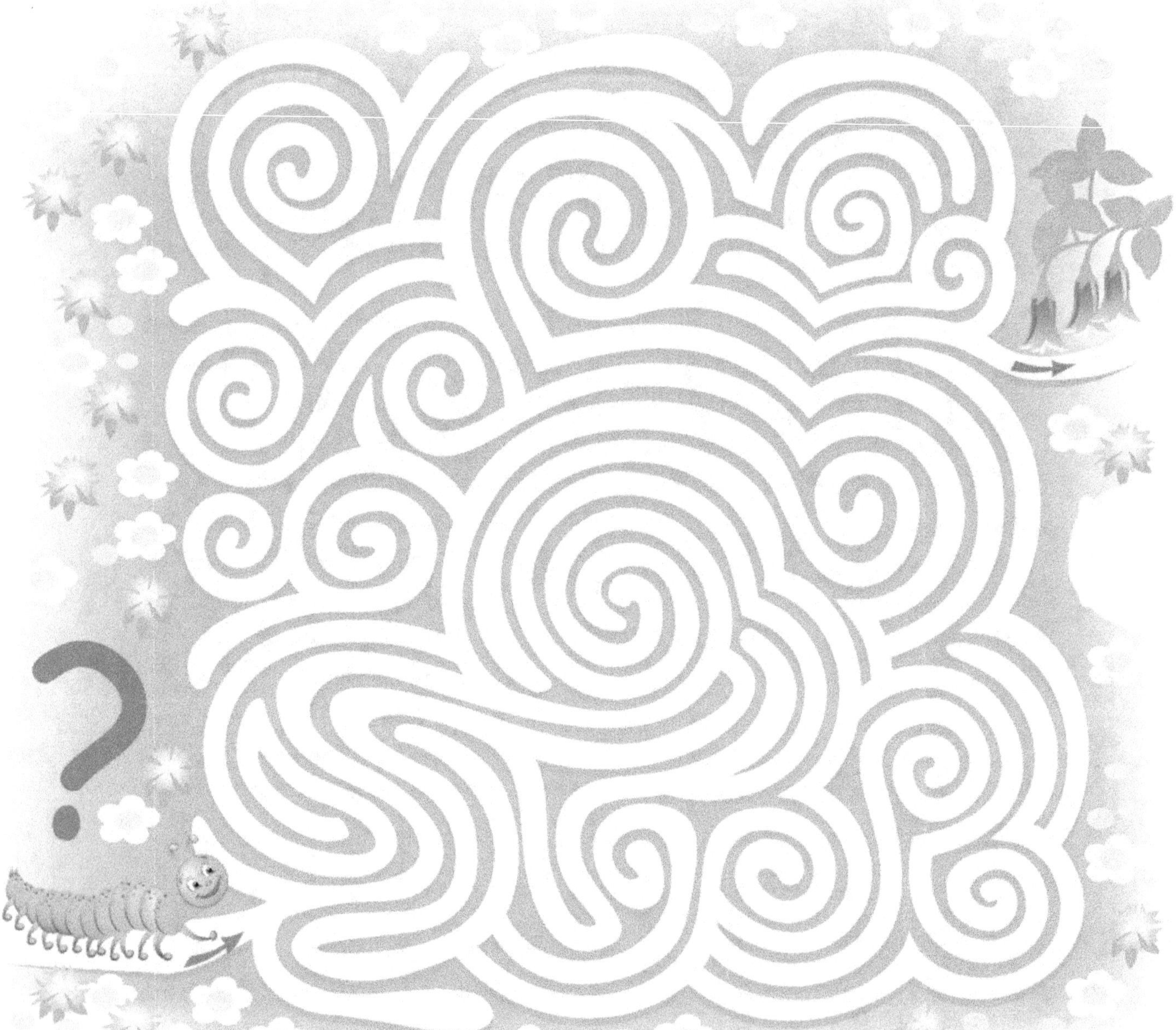

41

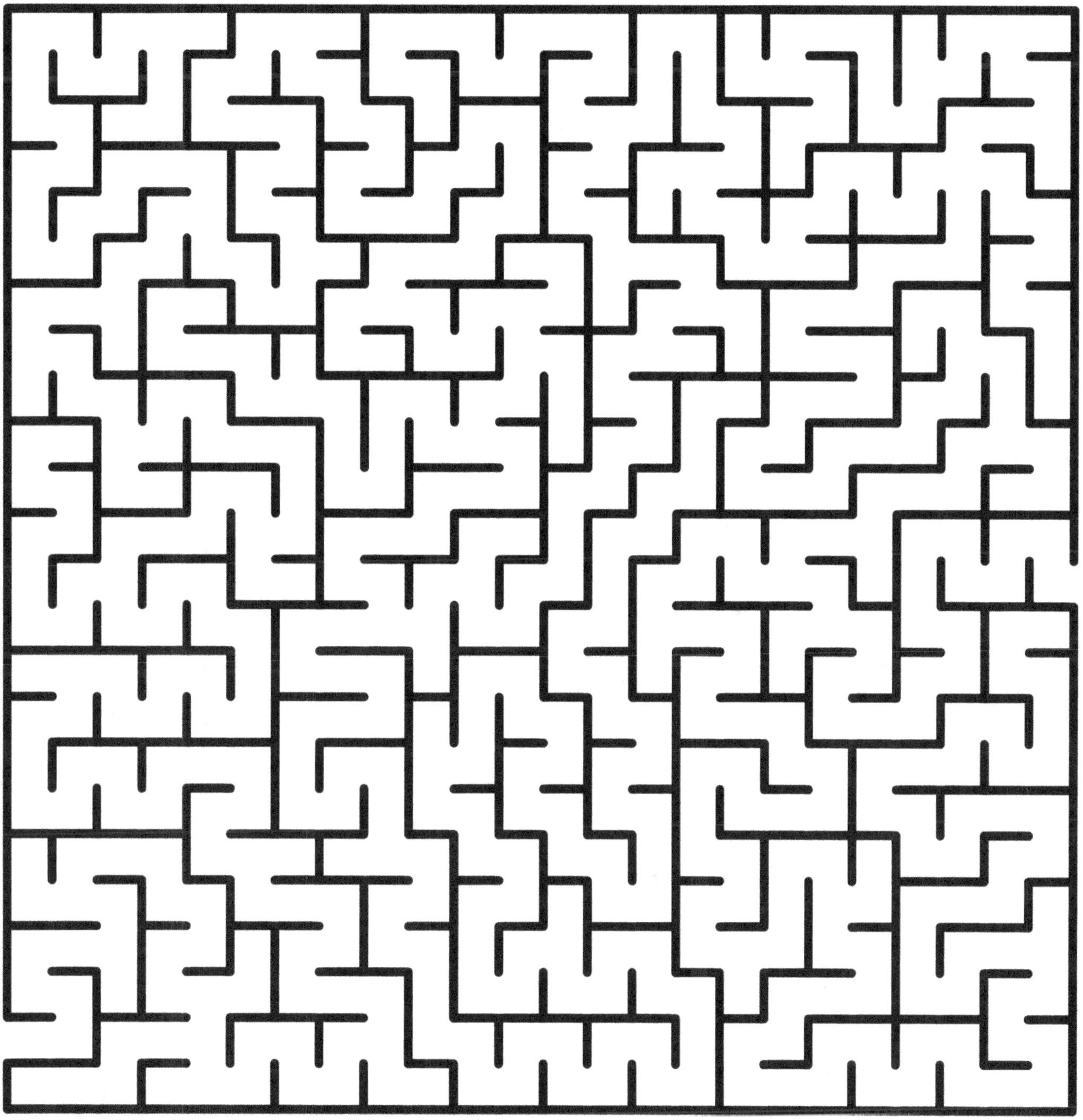

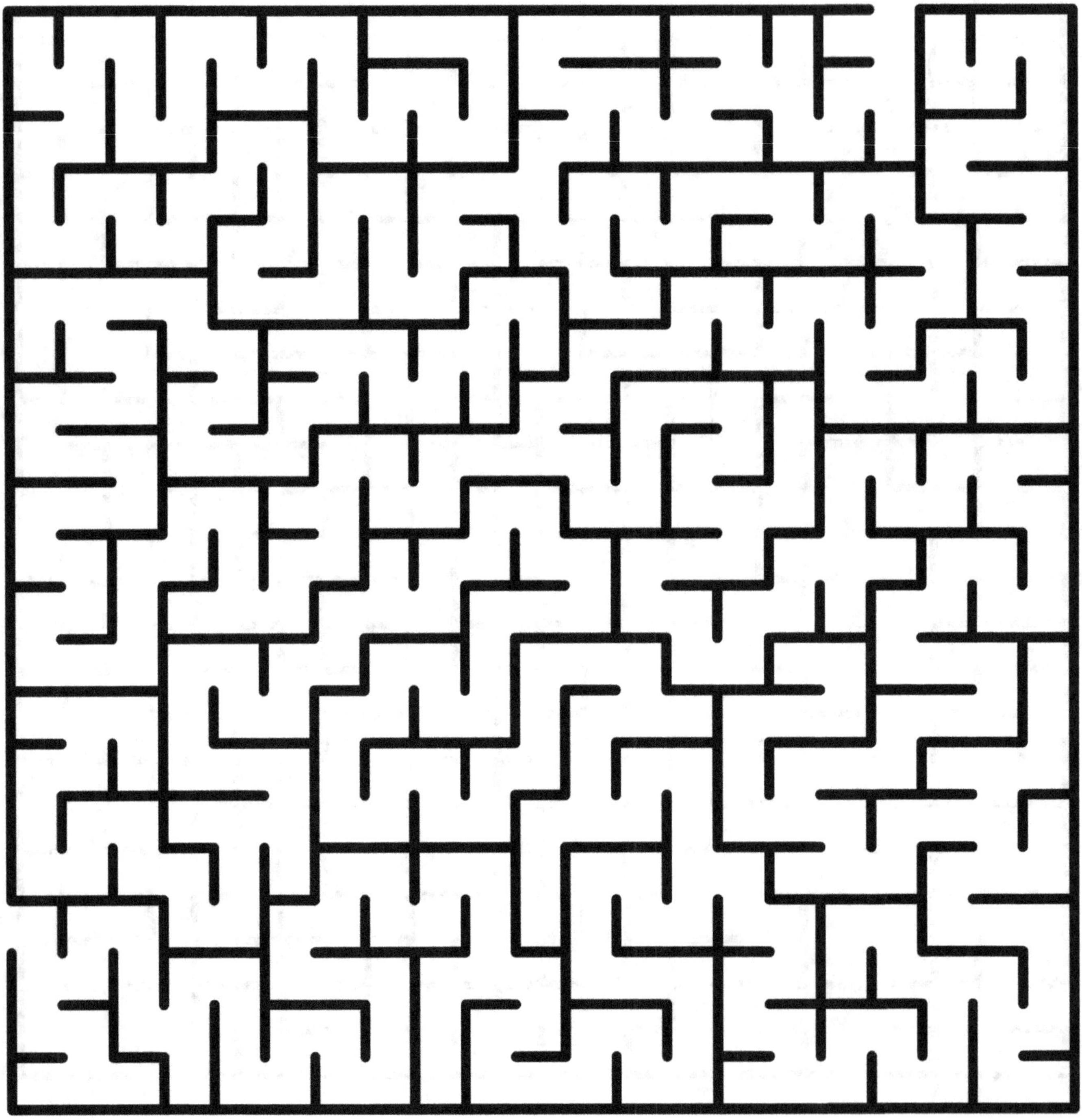

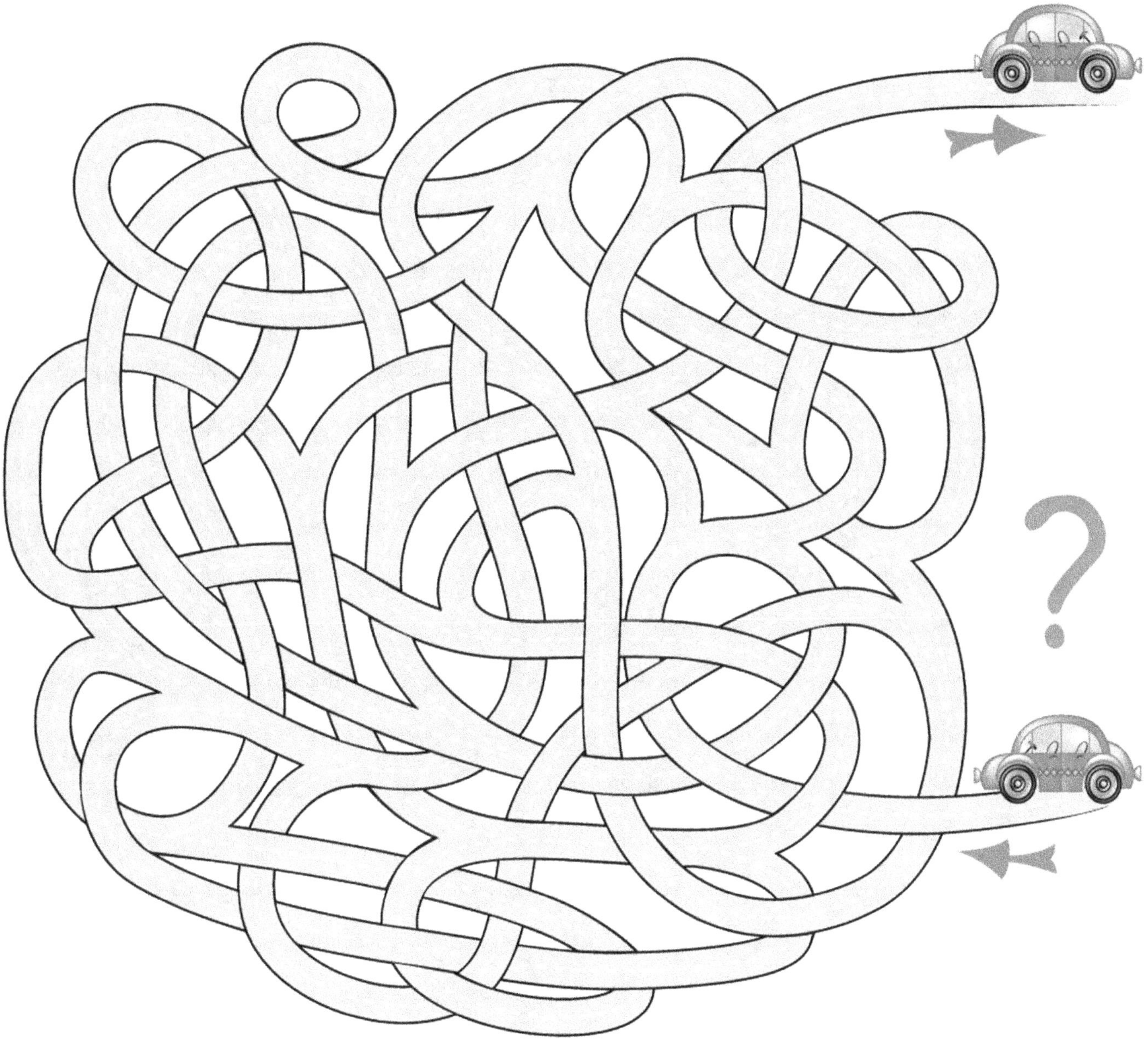

43

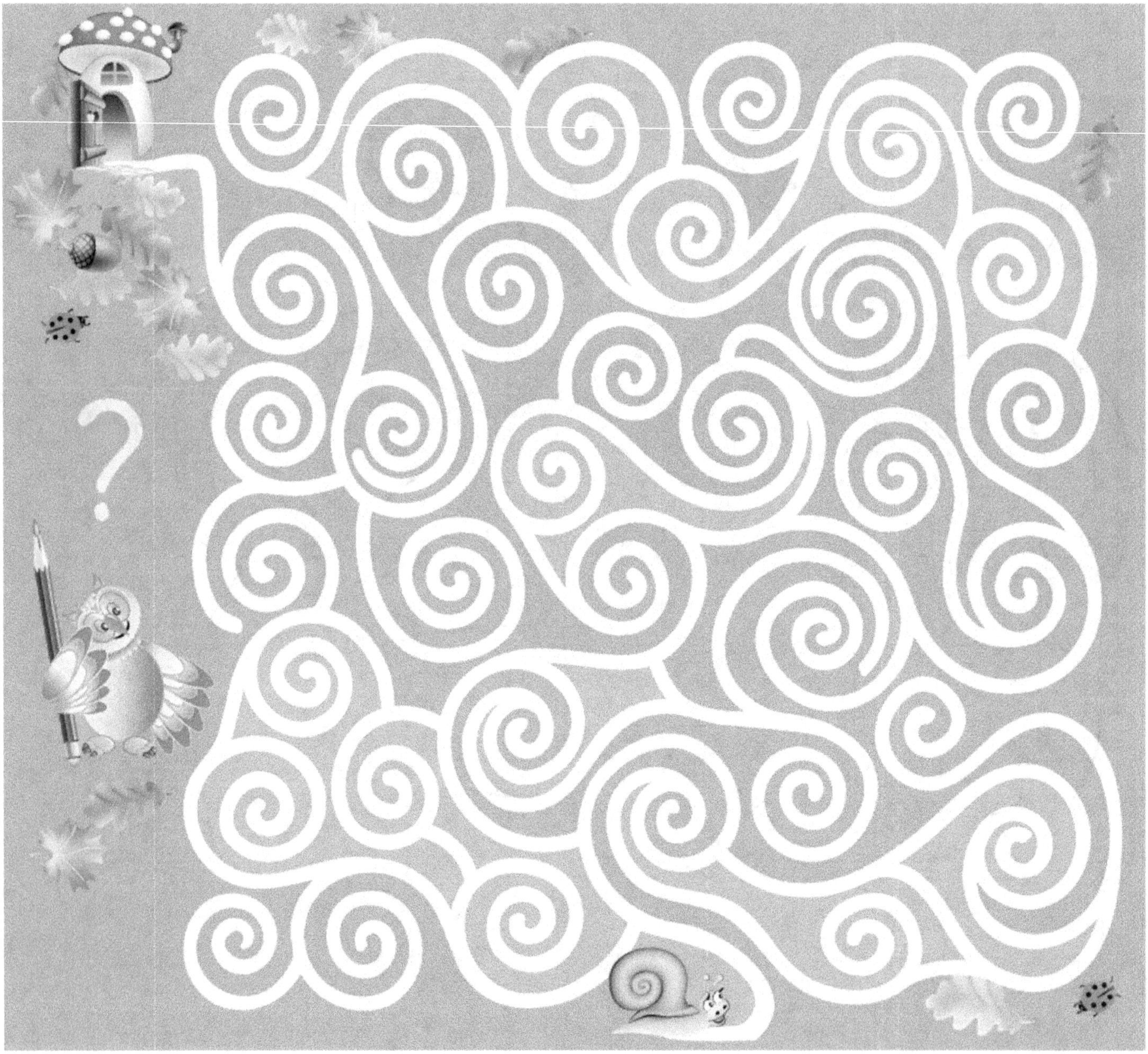

4

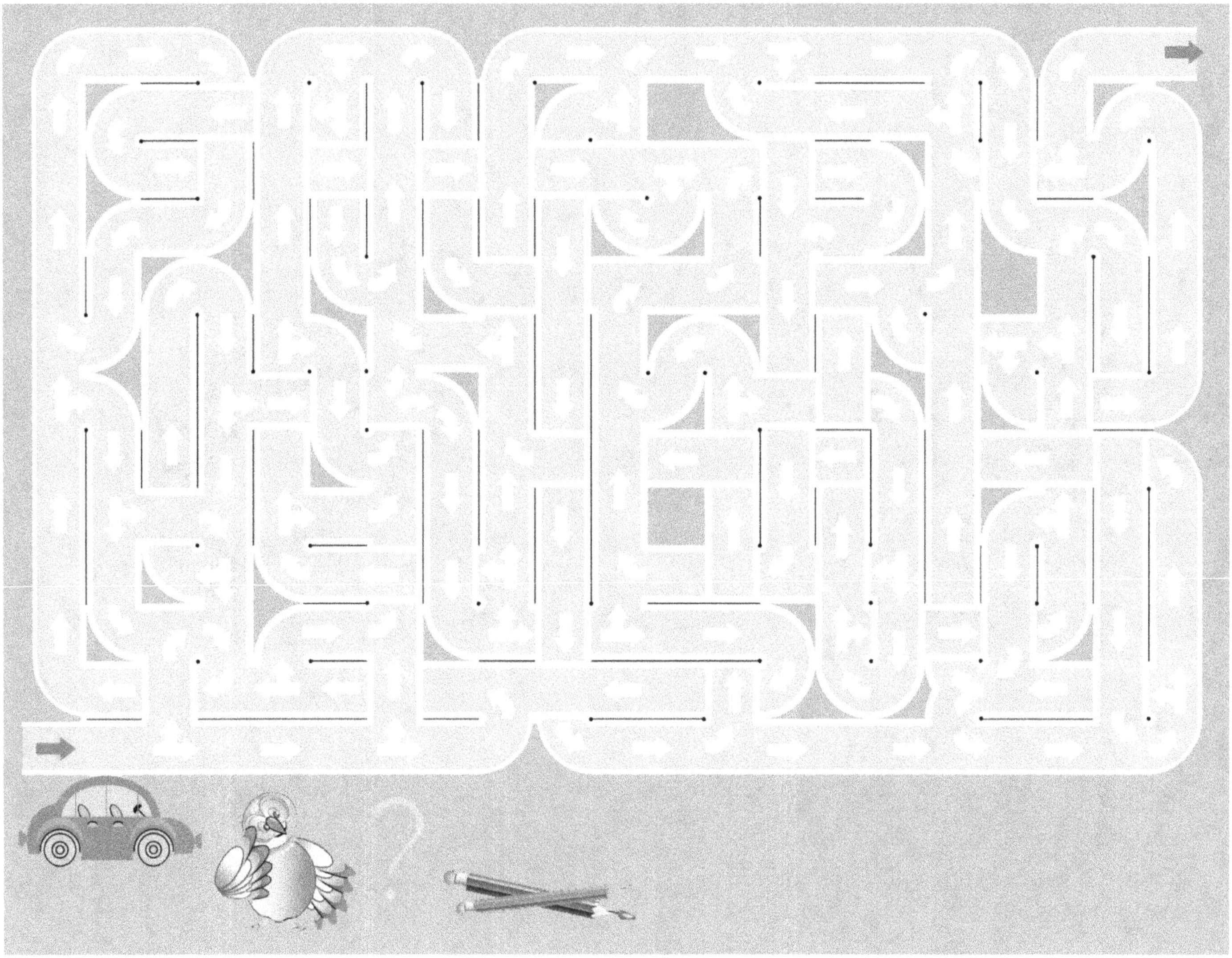

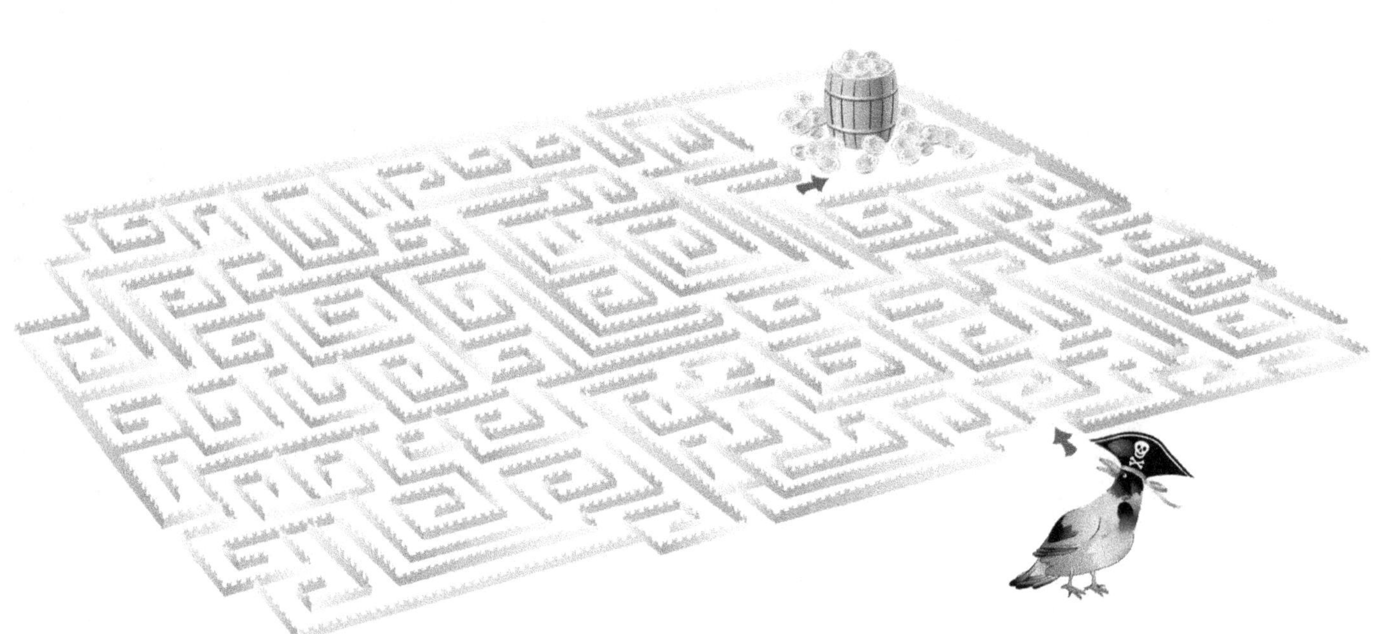

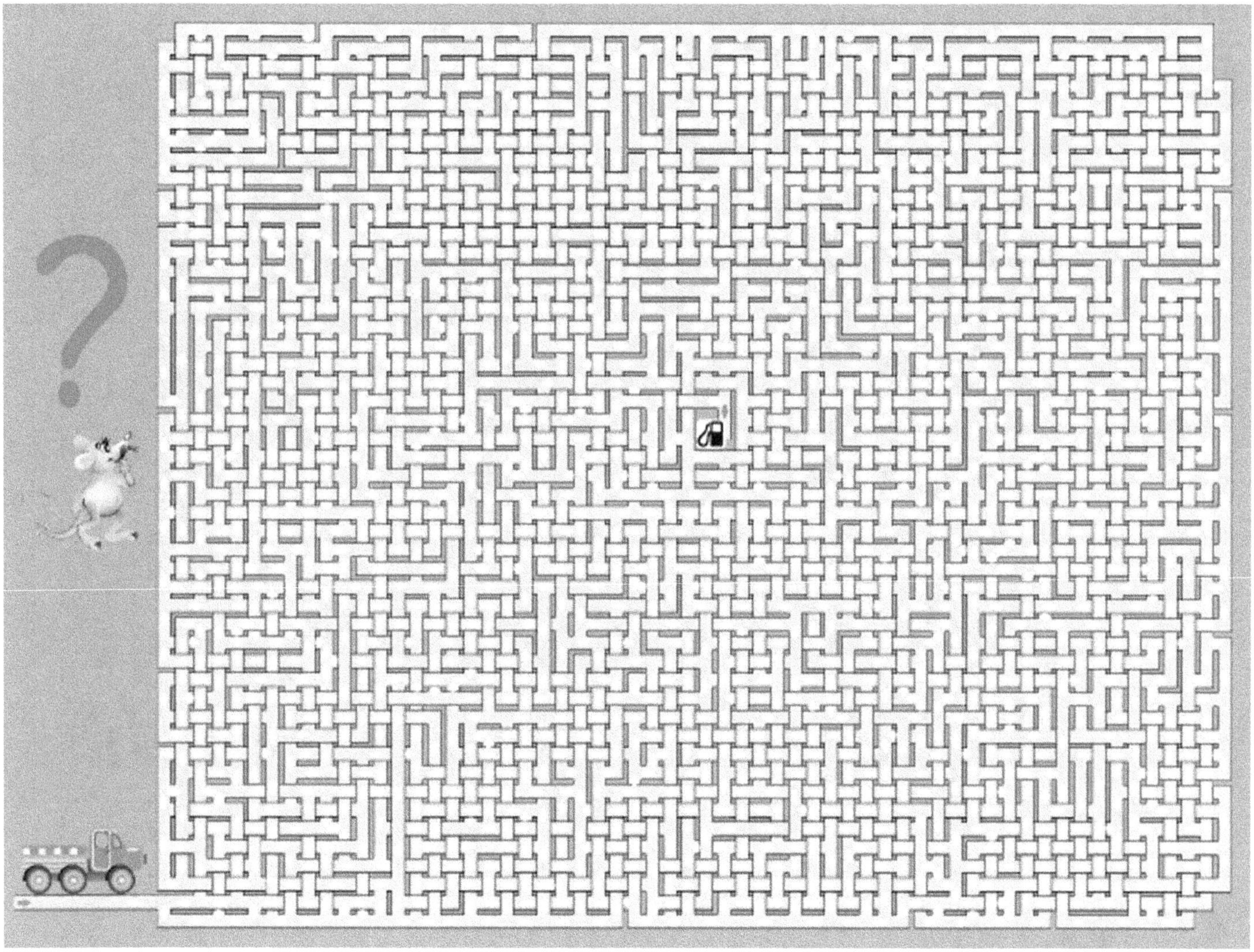

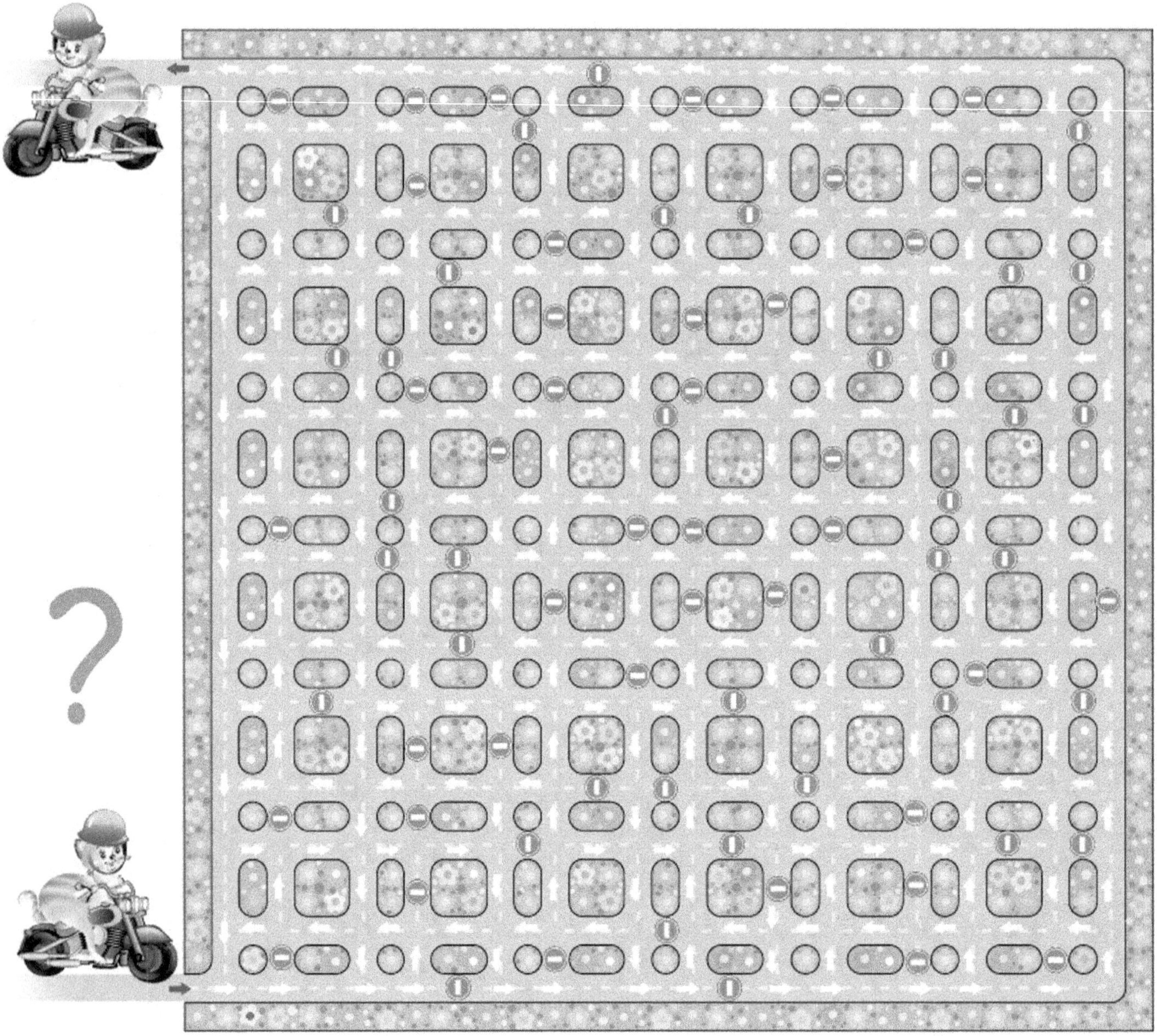

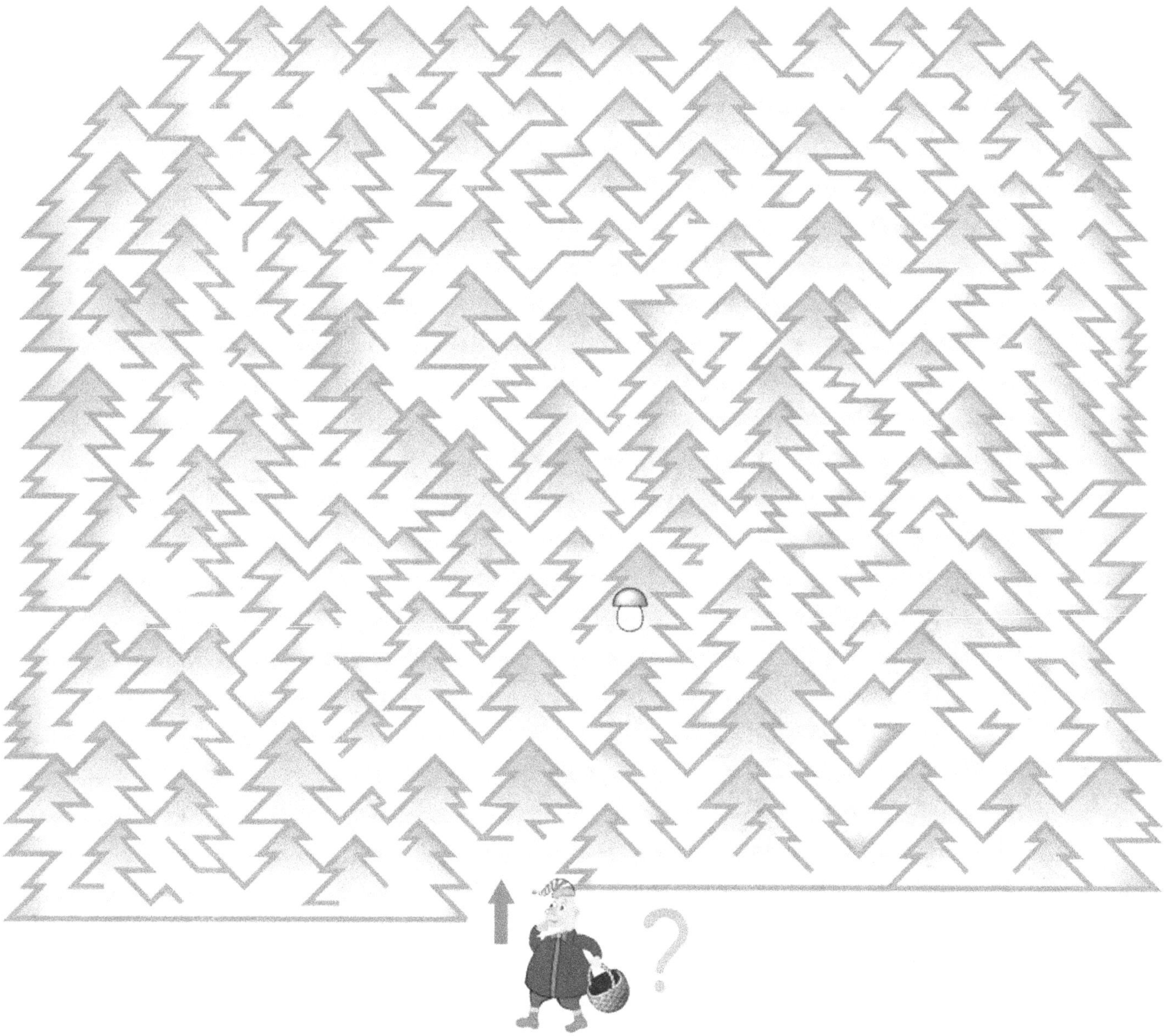

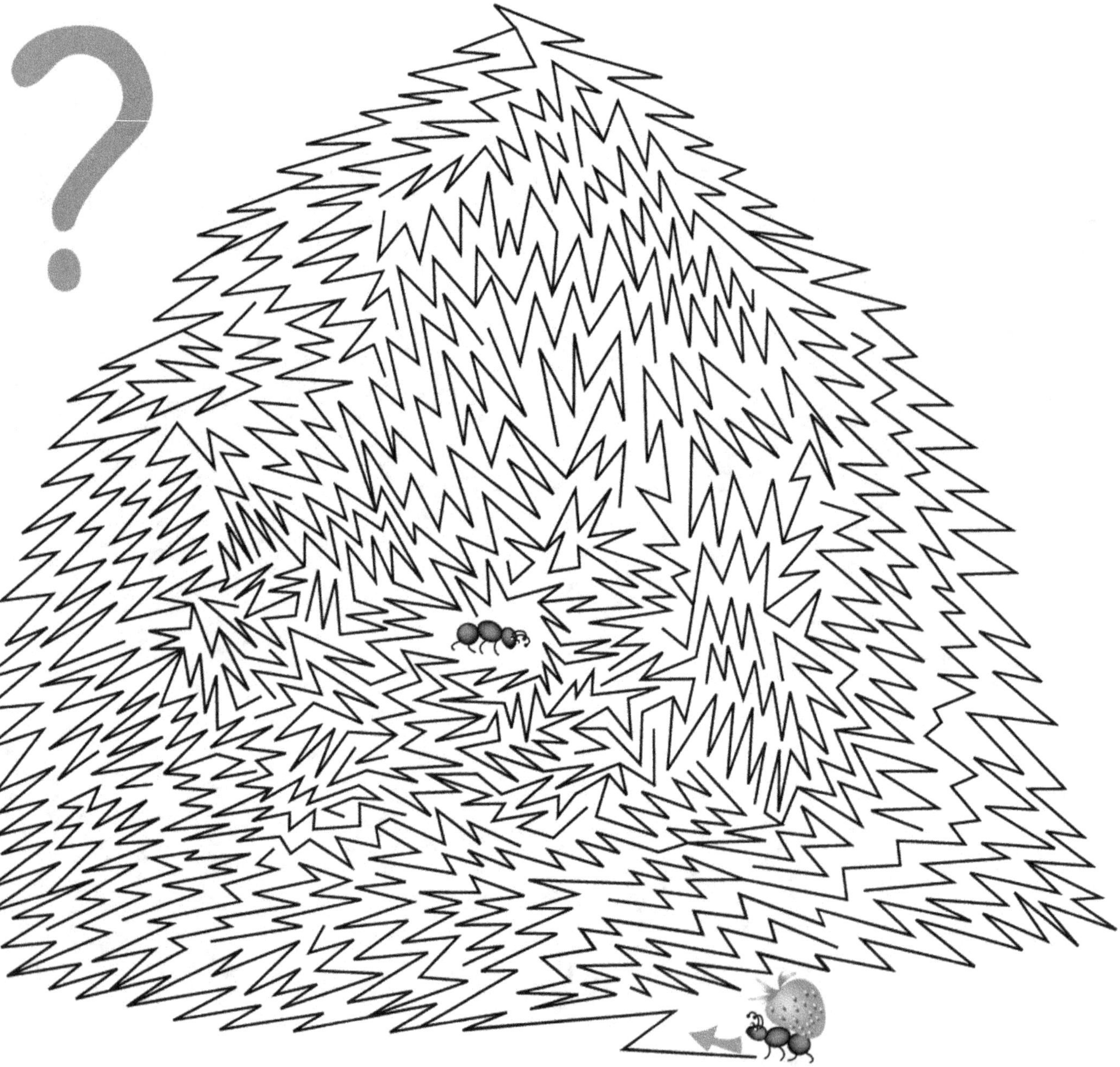

50

?

51

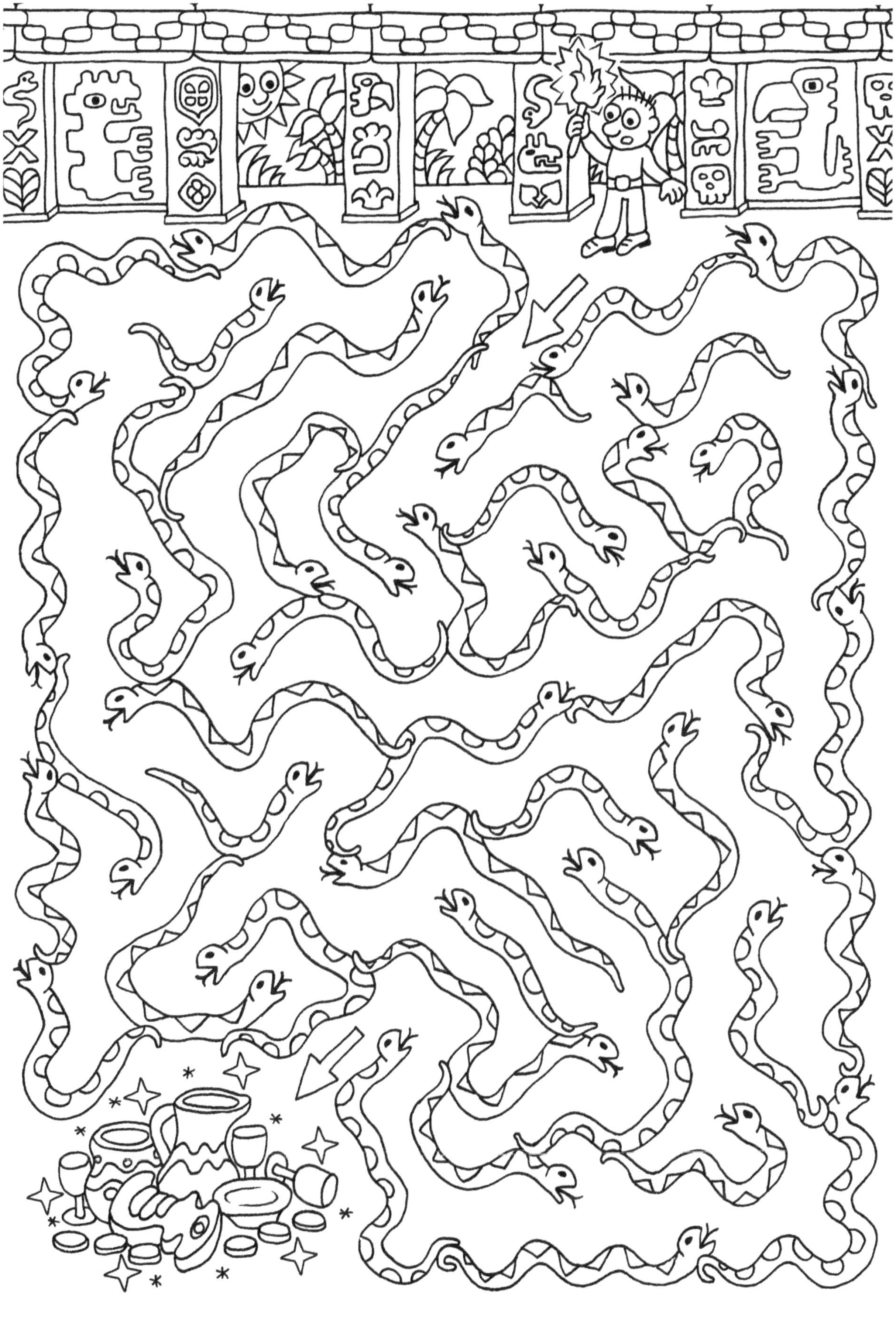

The key that you have can open only one locked door.
Can you get out of the maze?

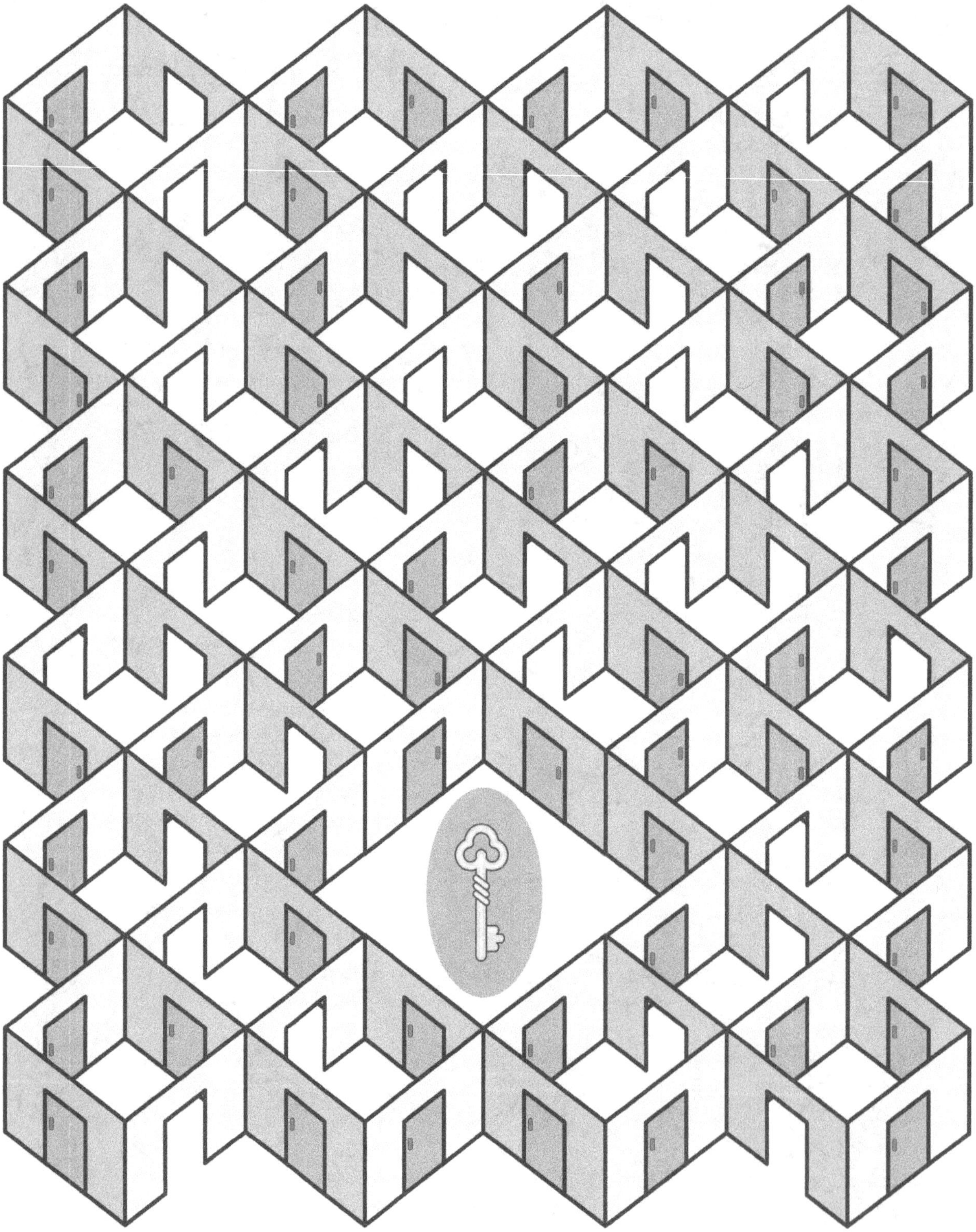

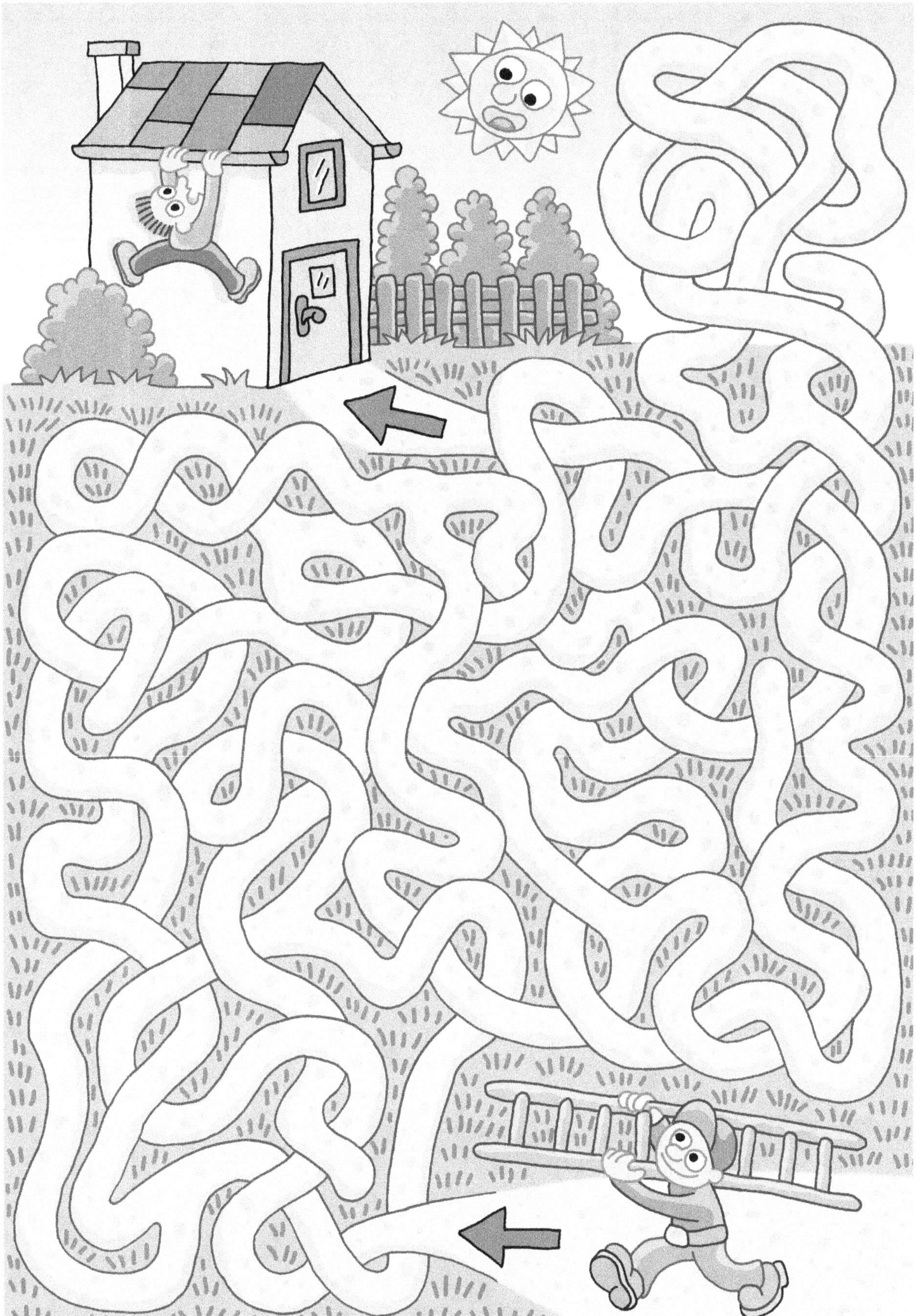

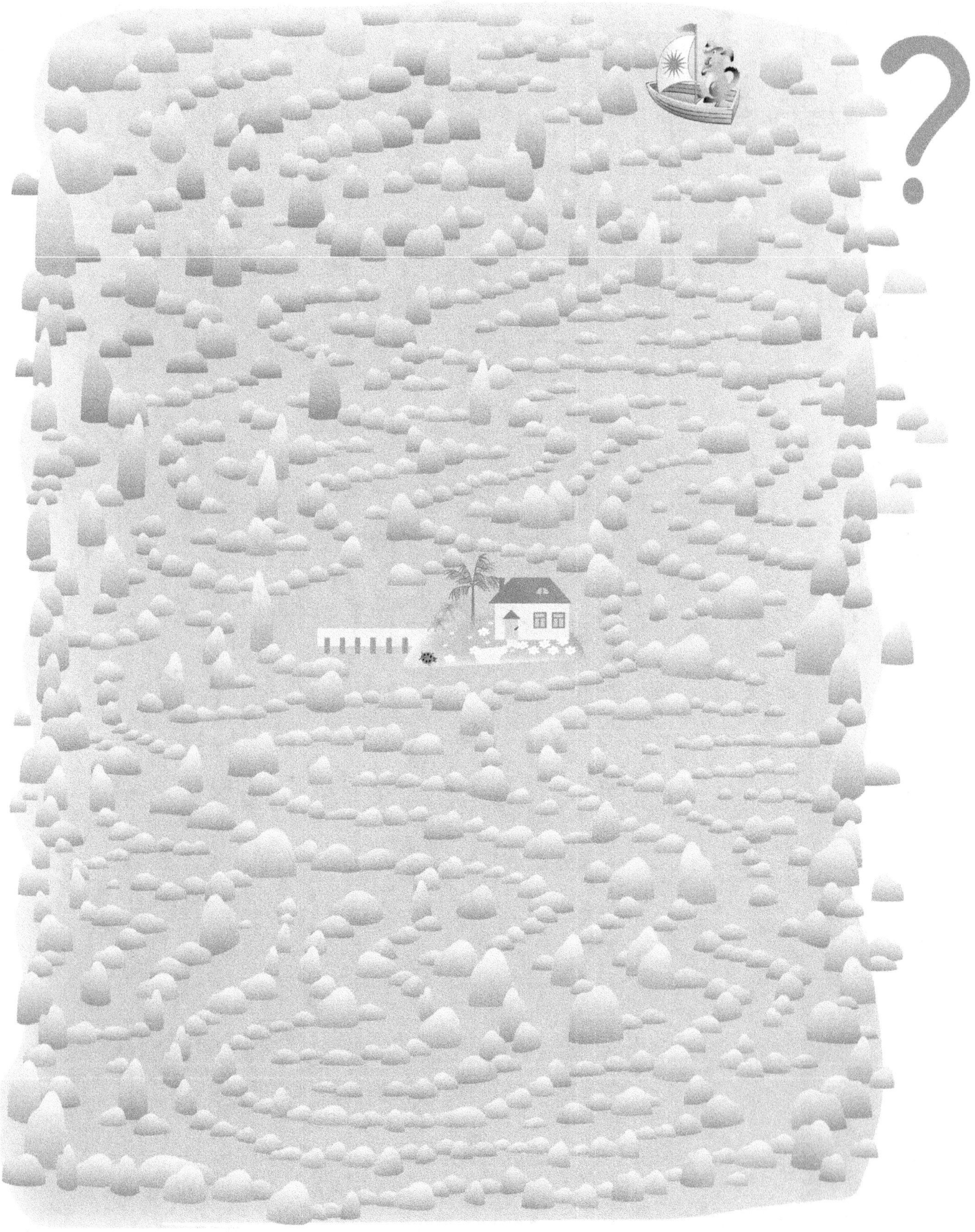

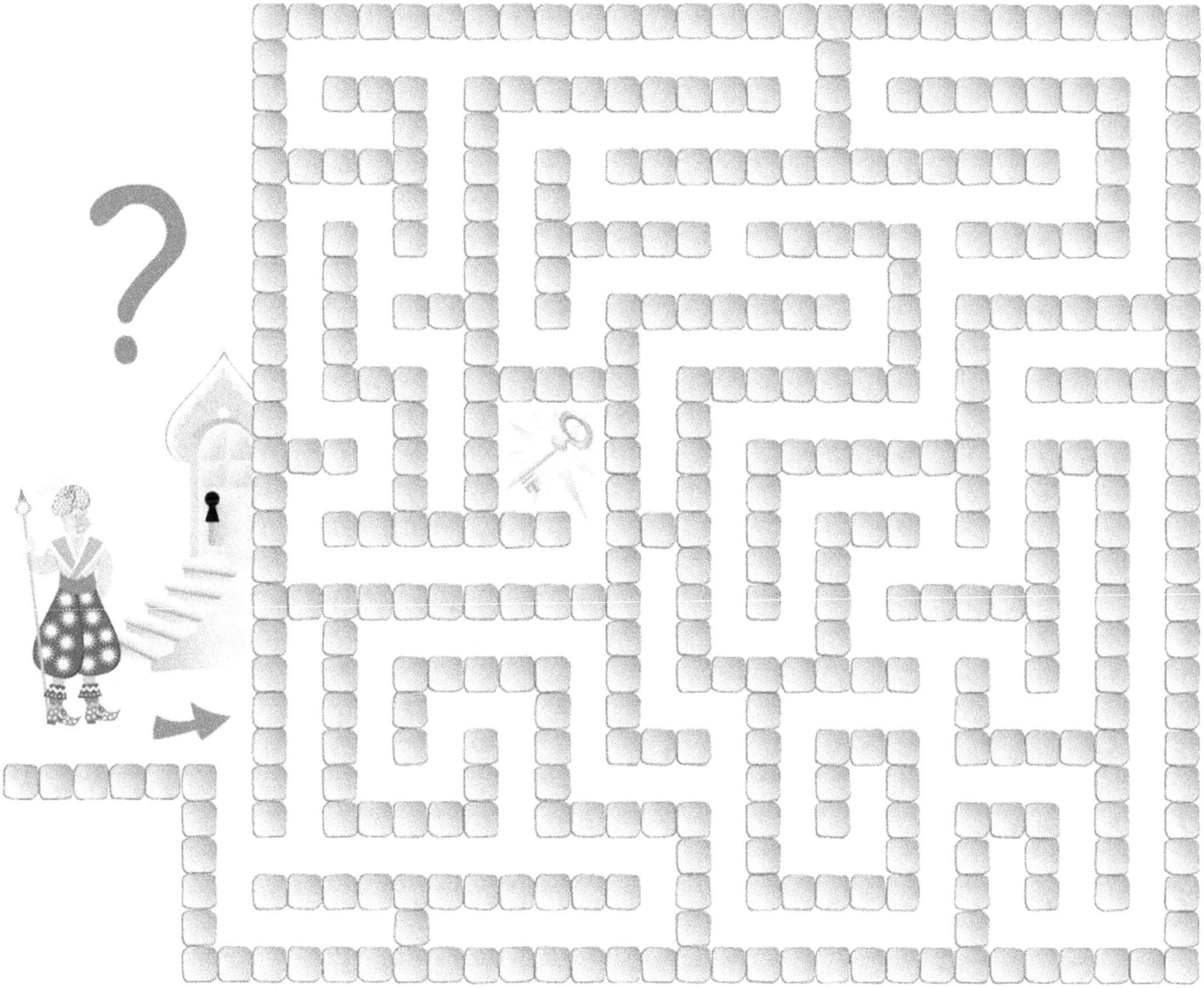

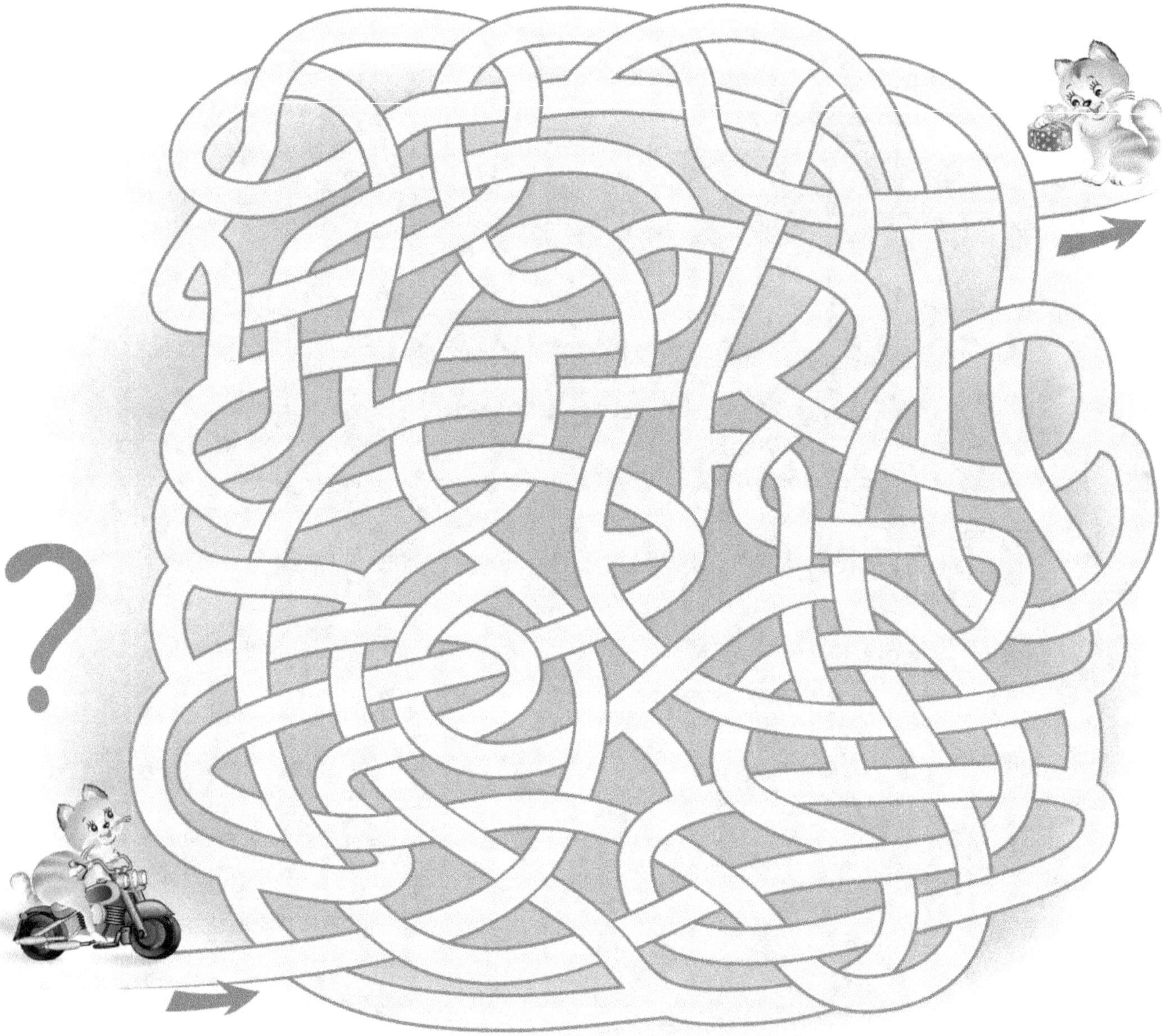

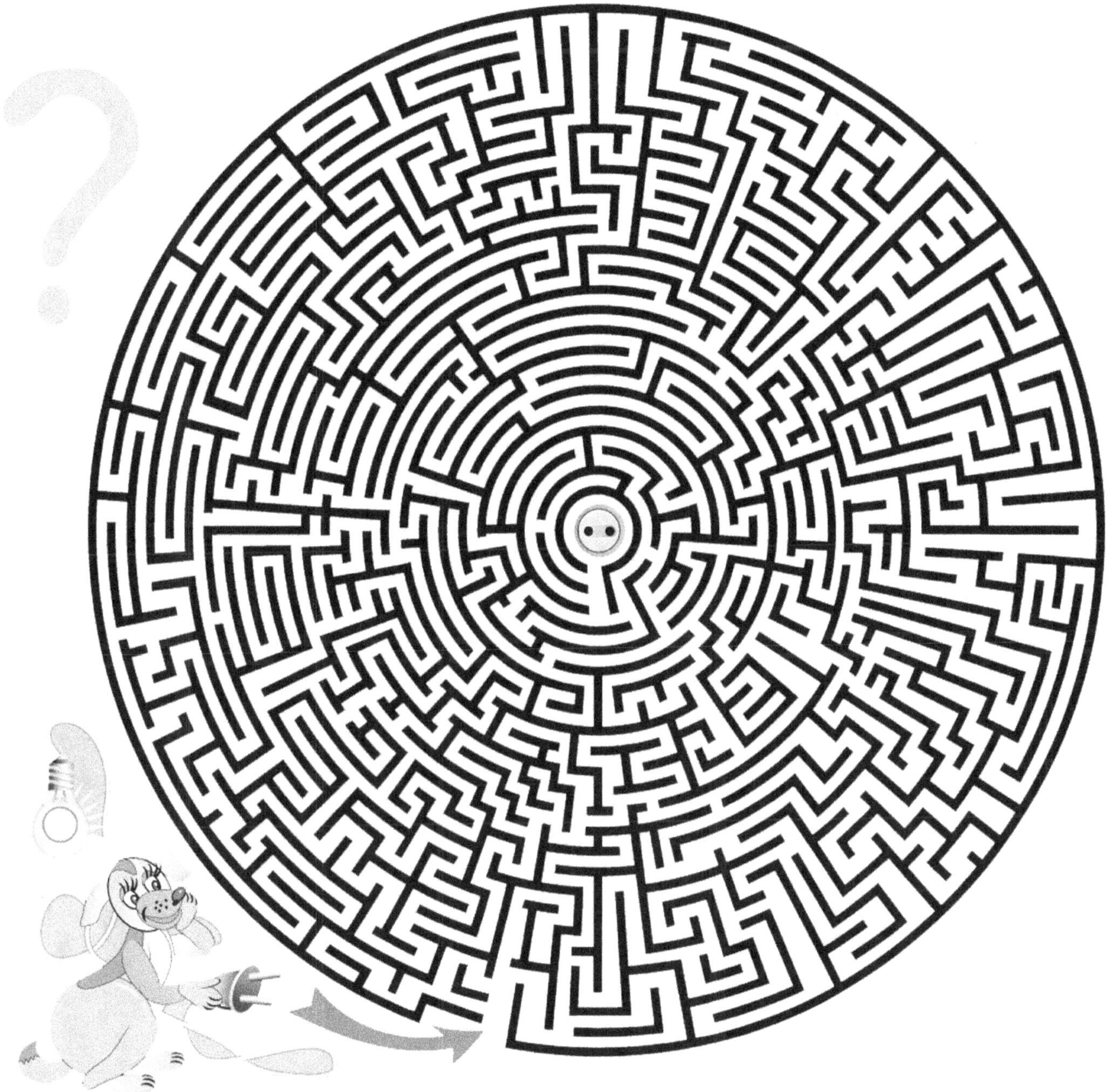

57

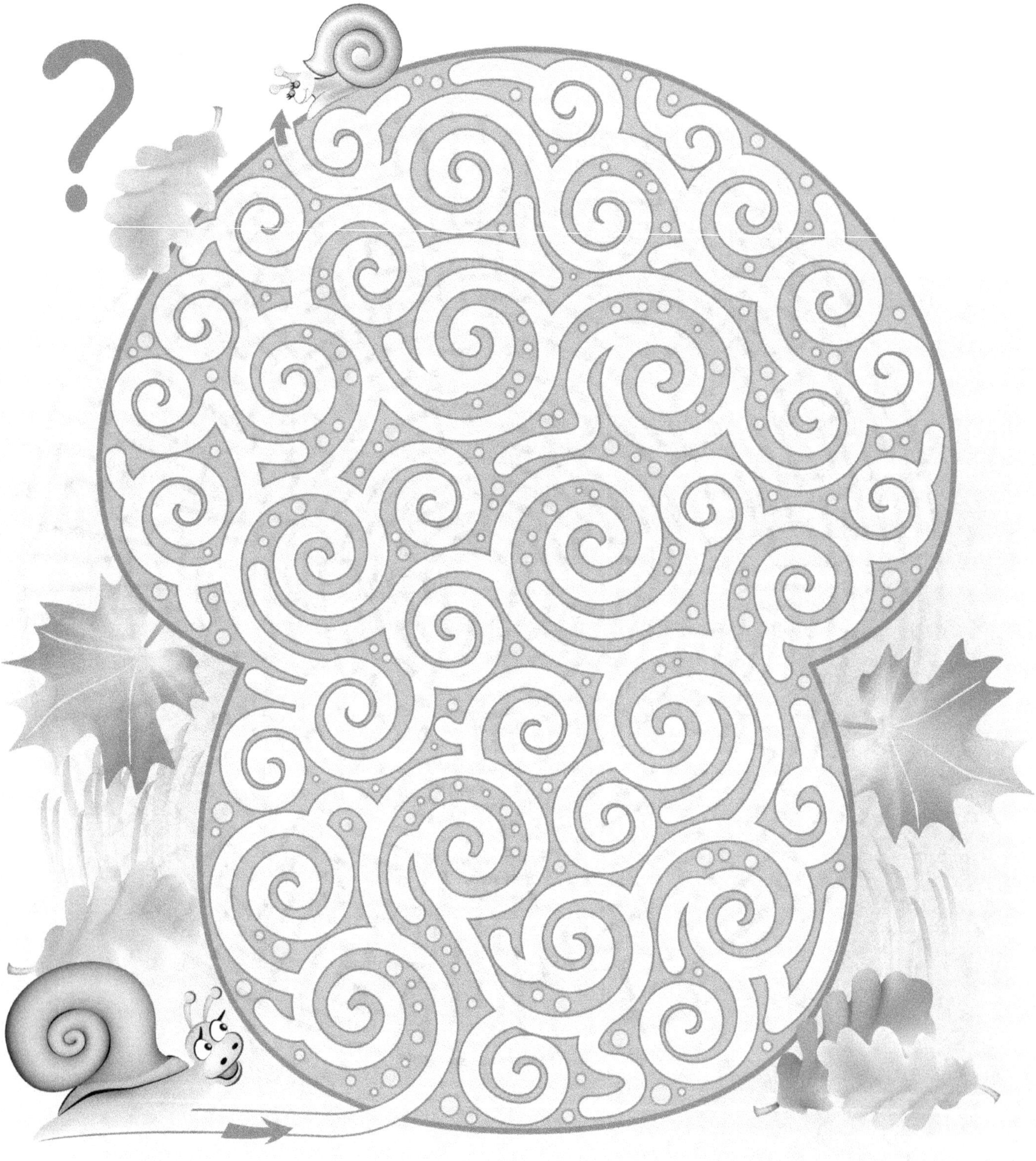

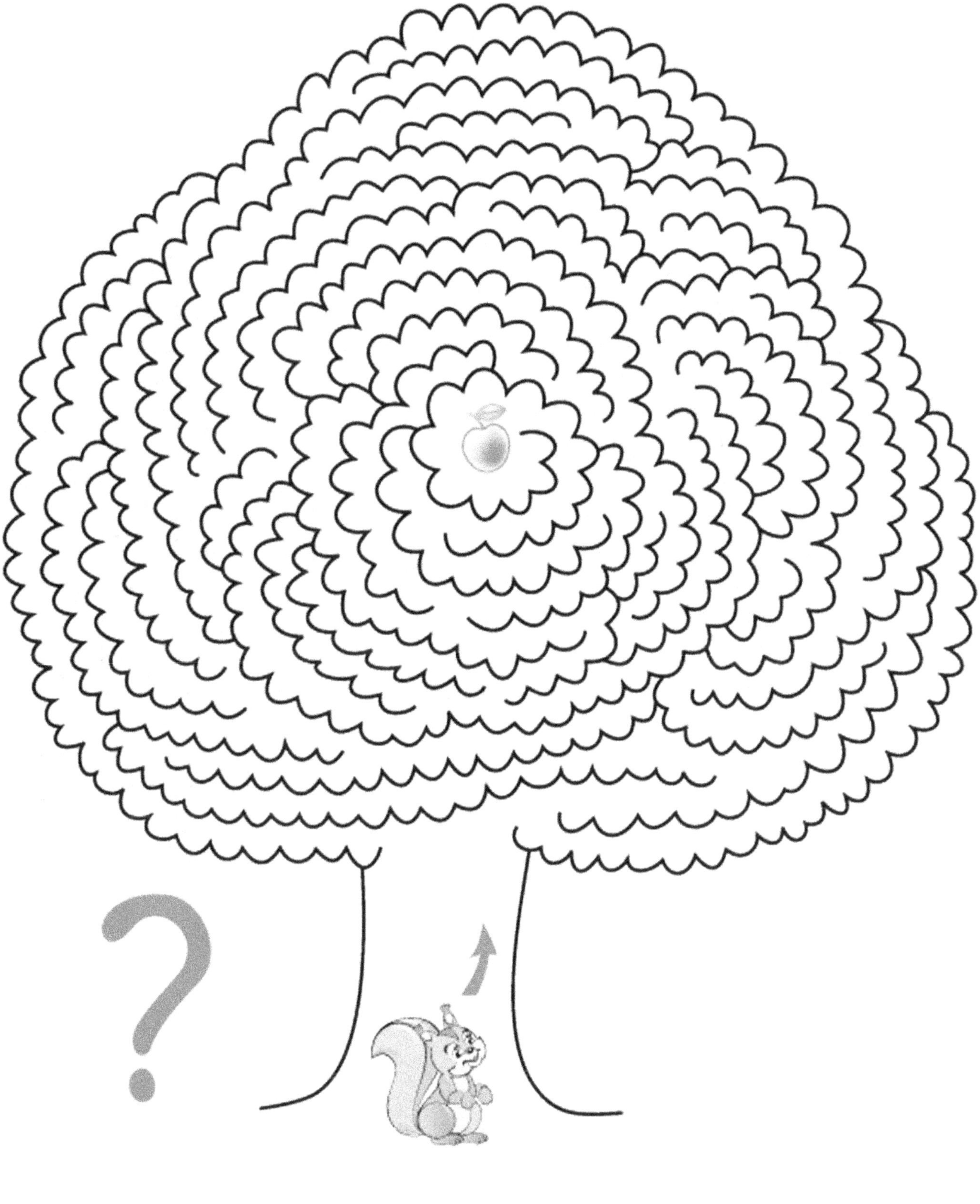

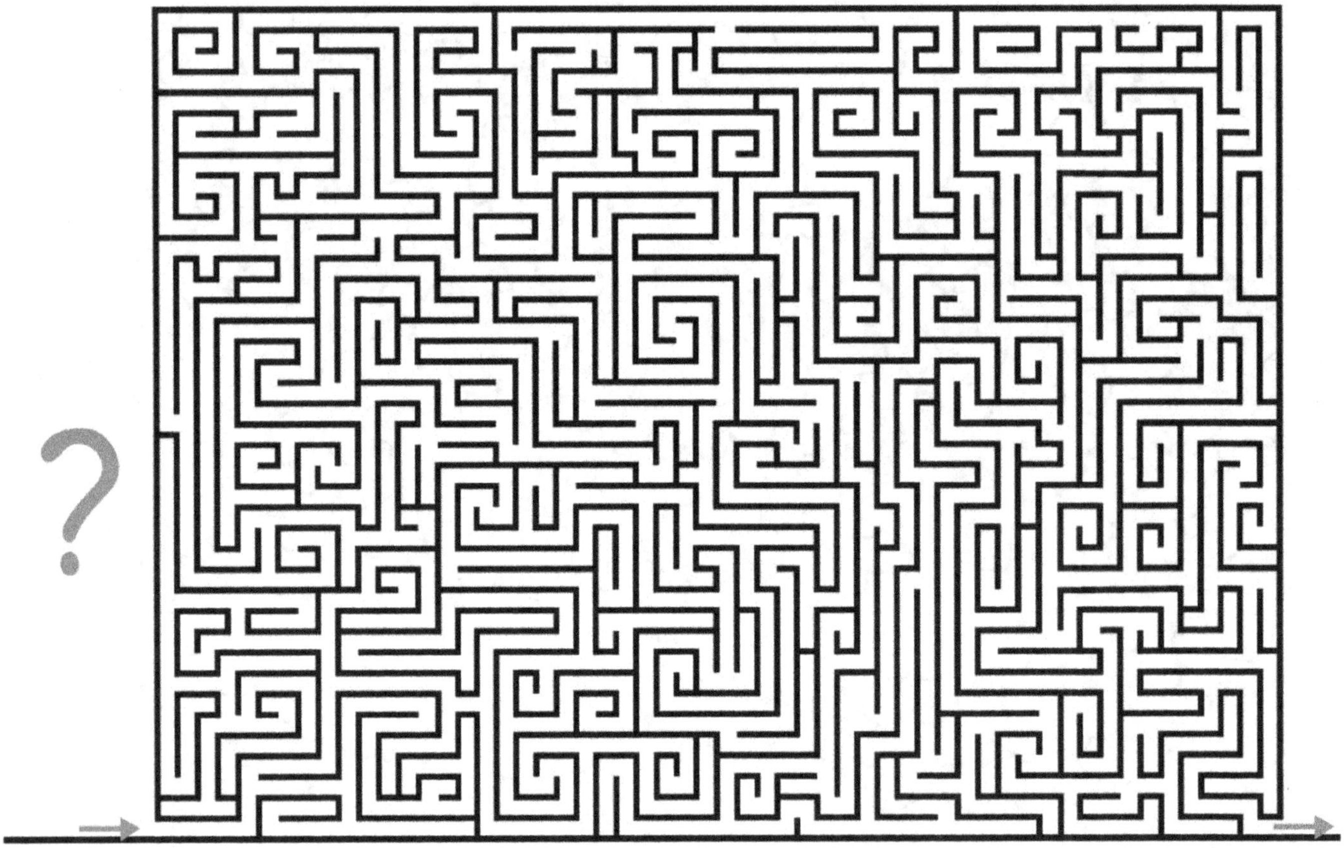

HOTEL

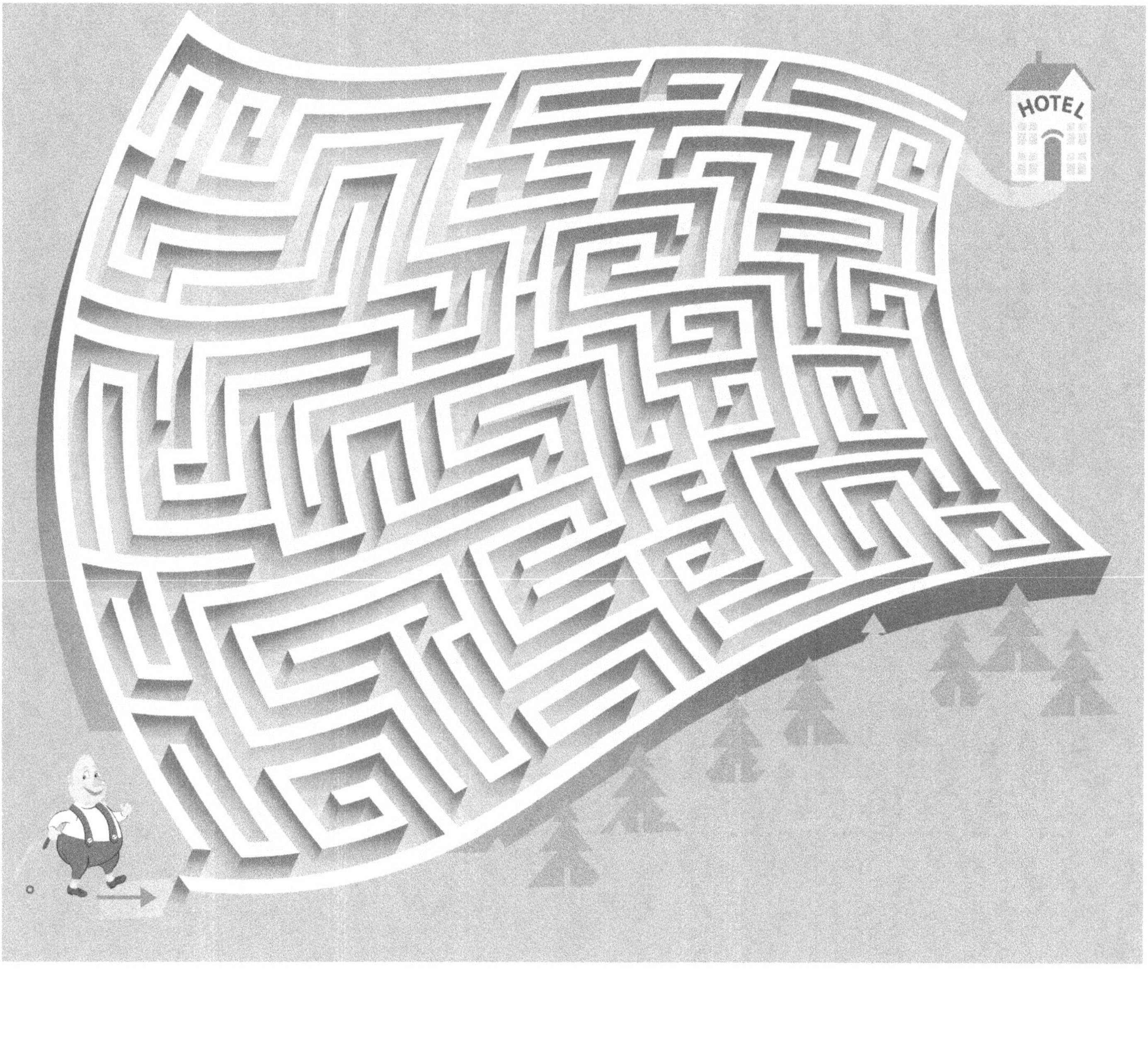

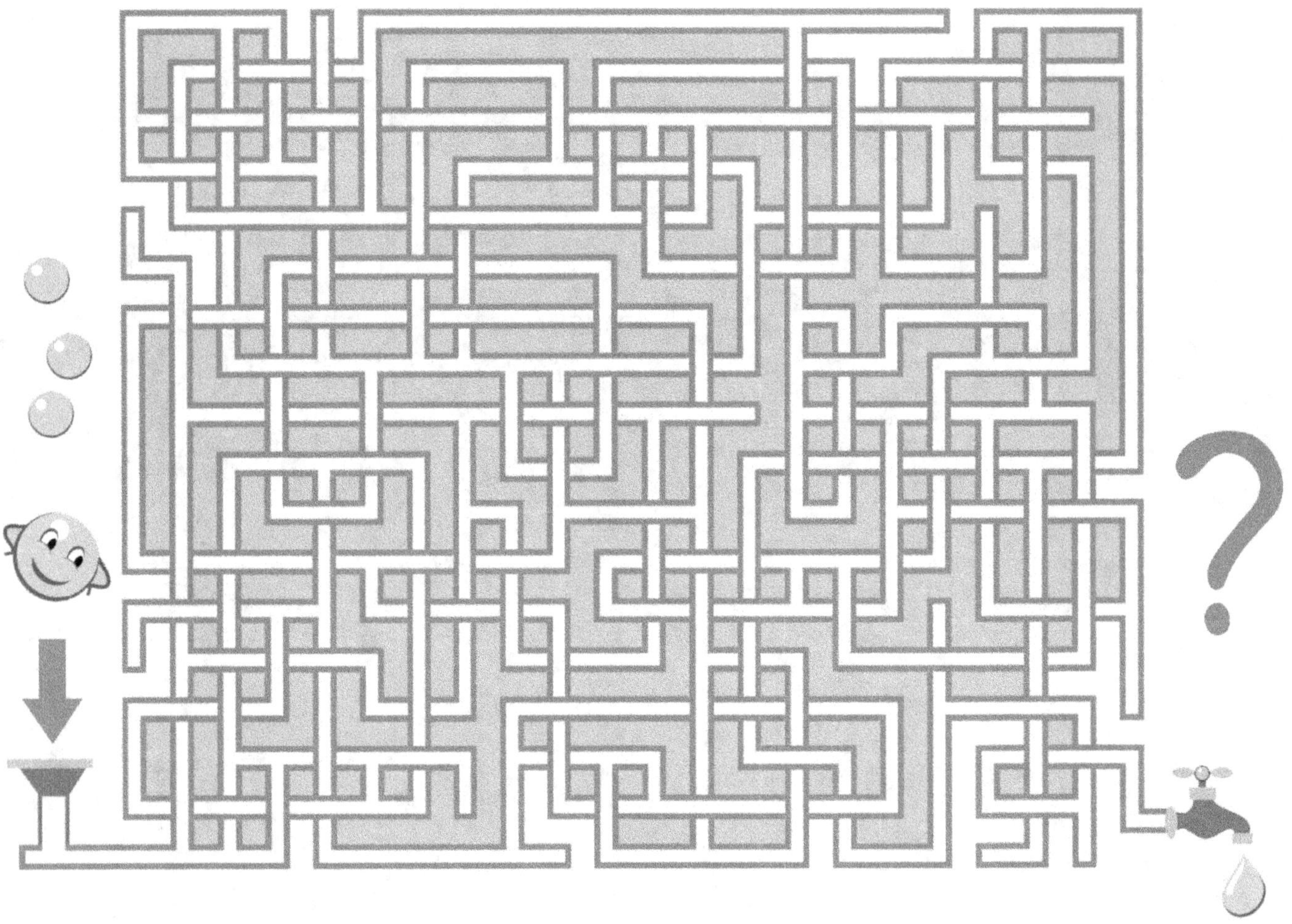

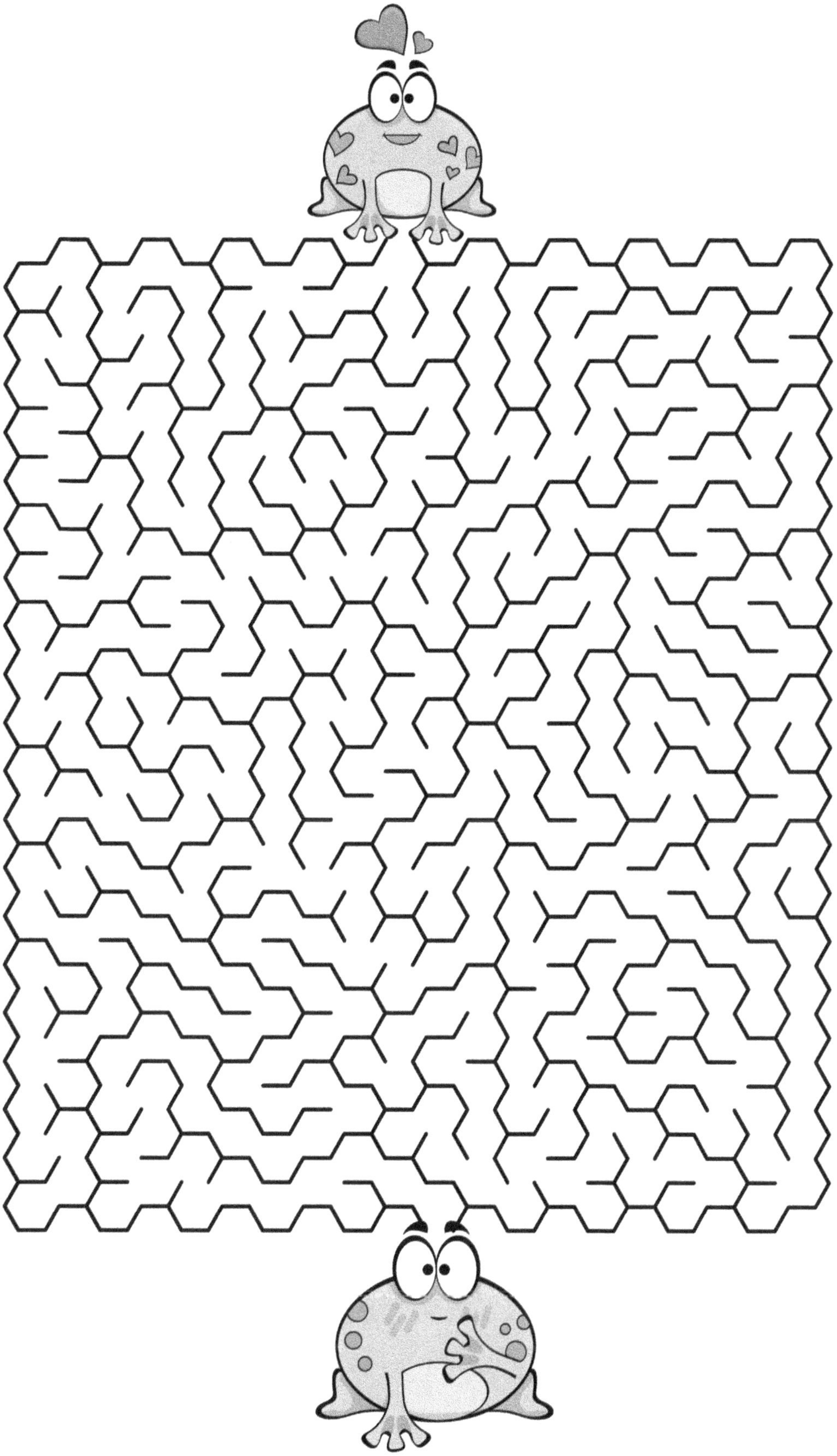

61

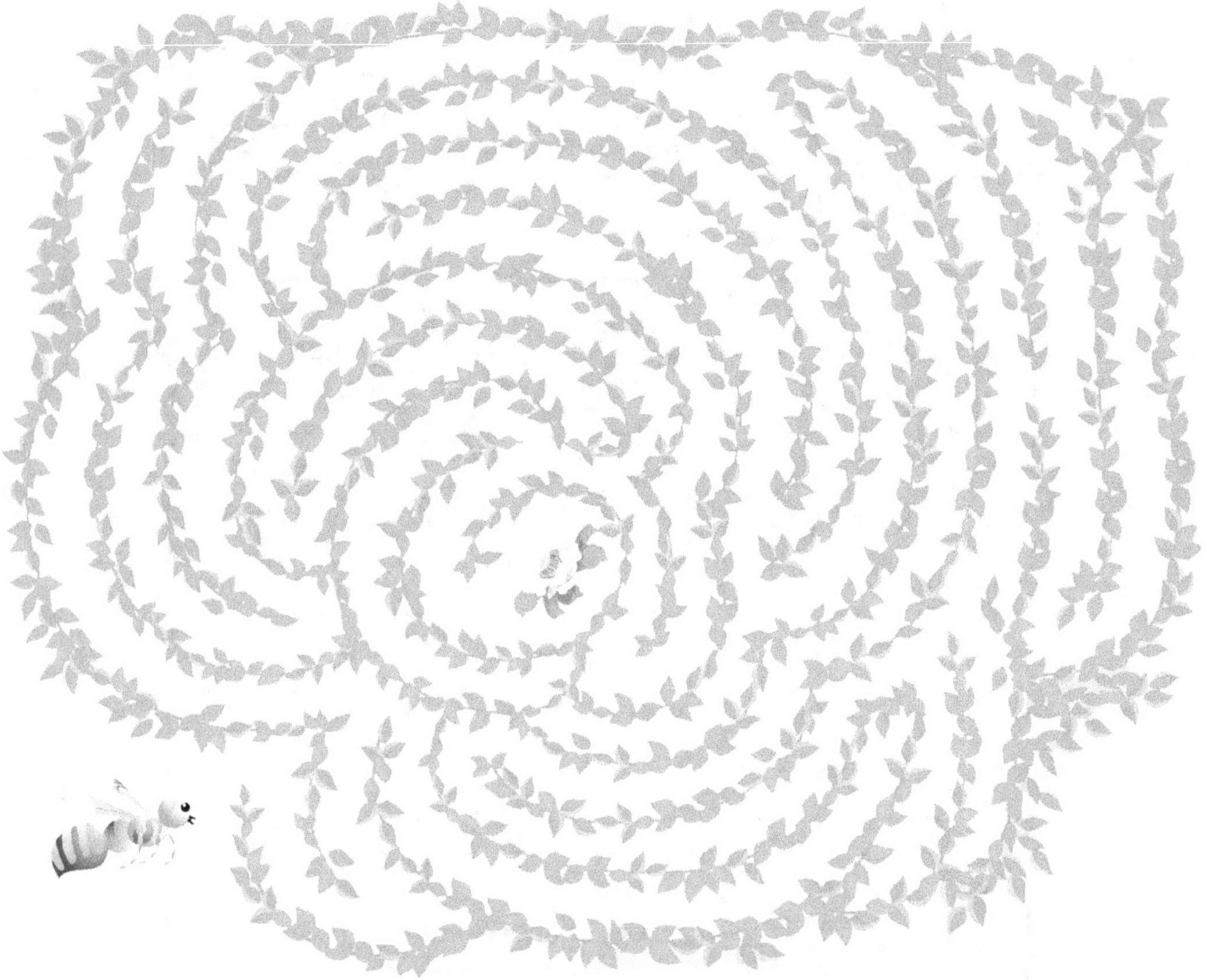

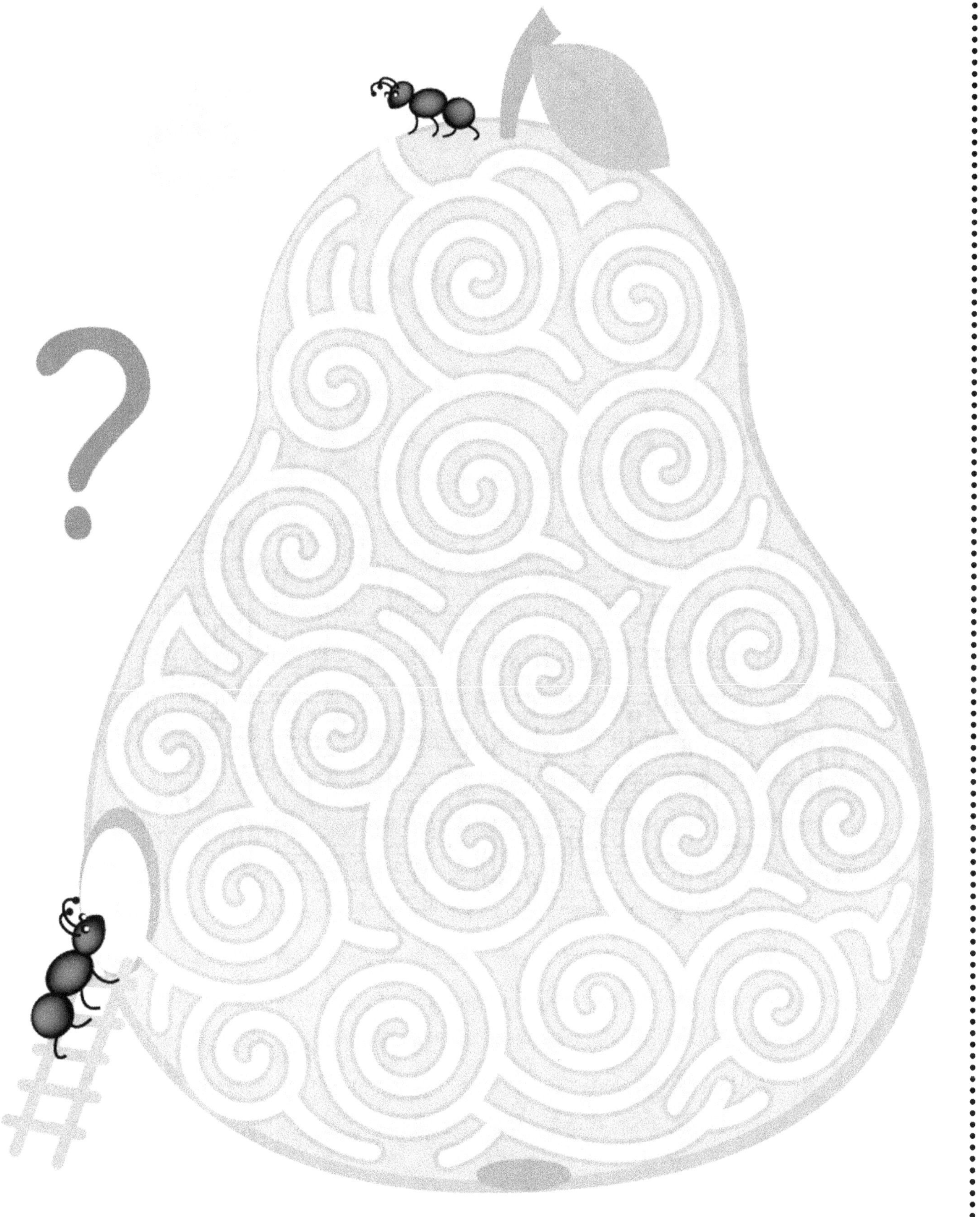

66

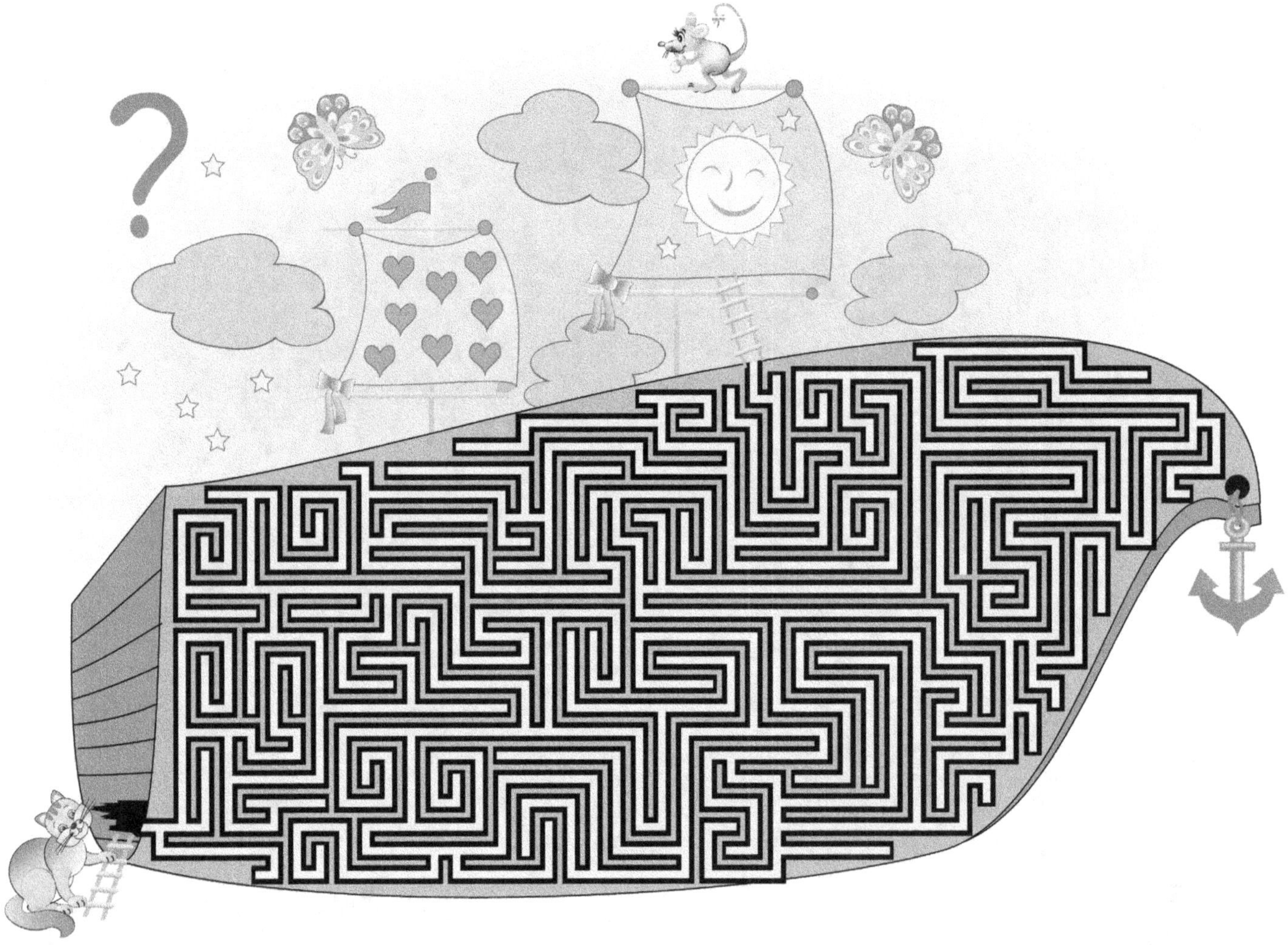

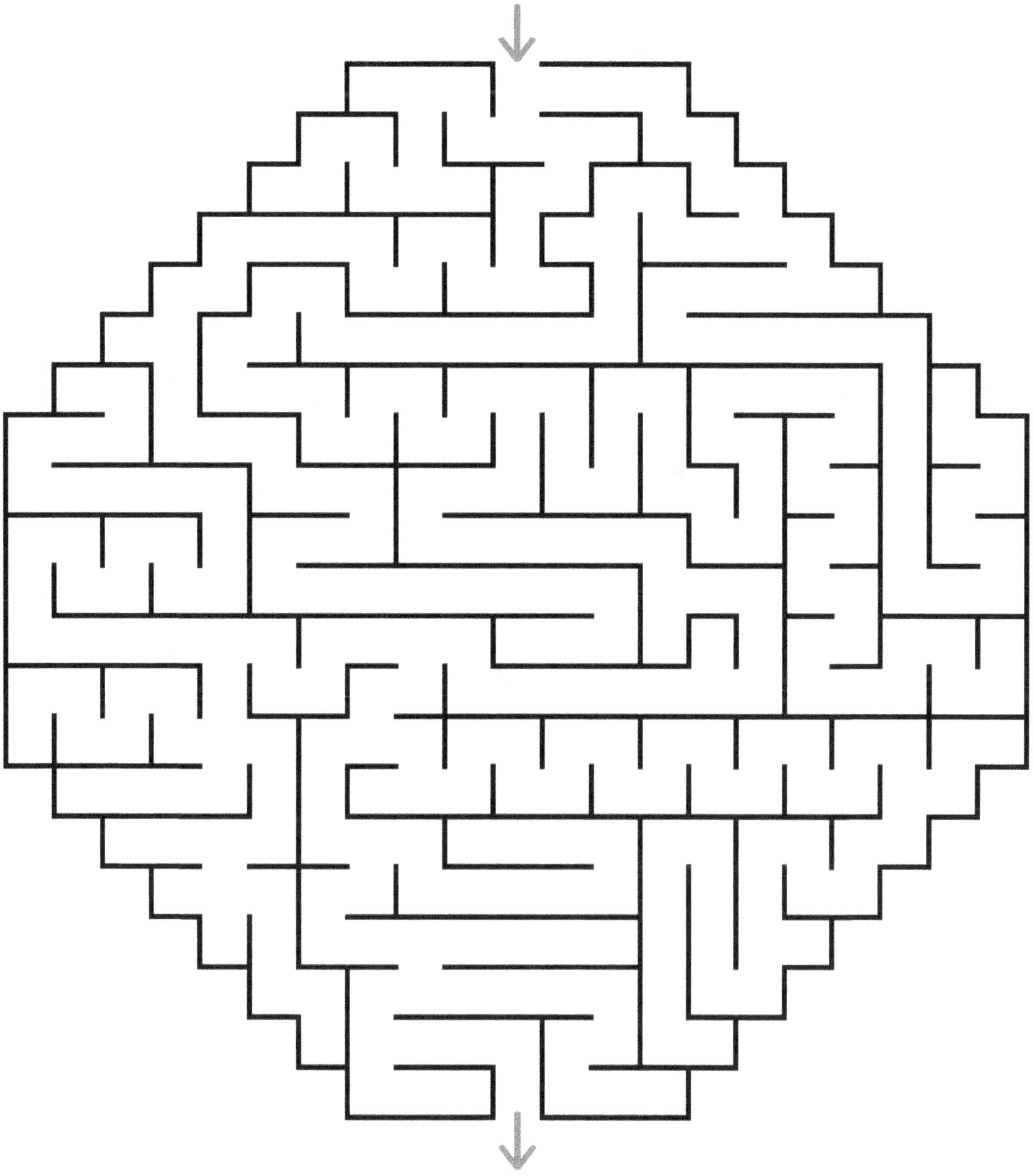

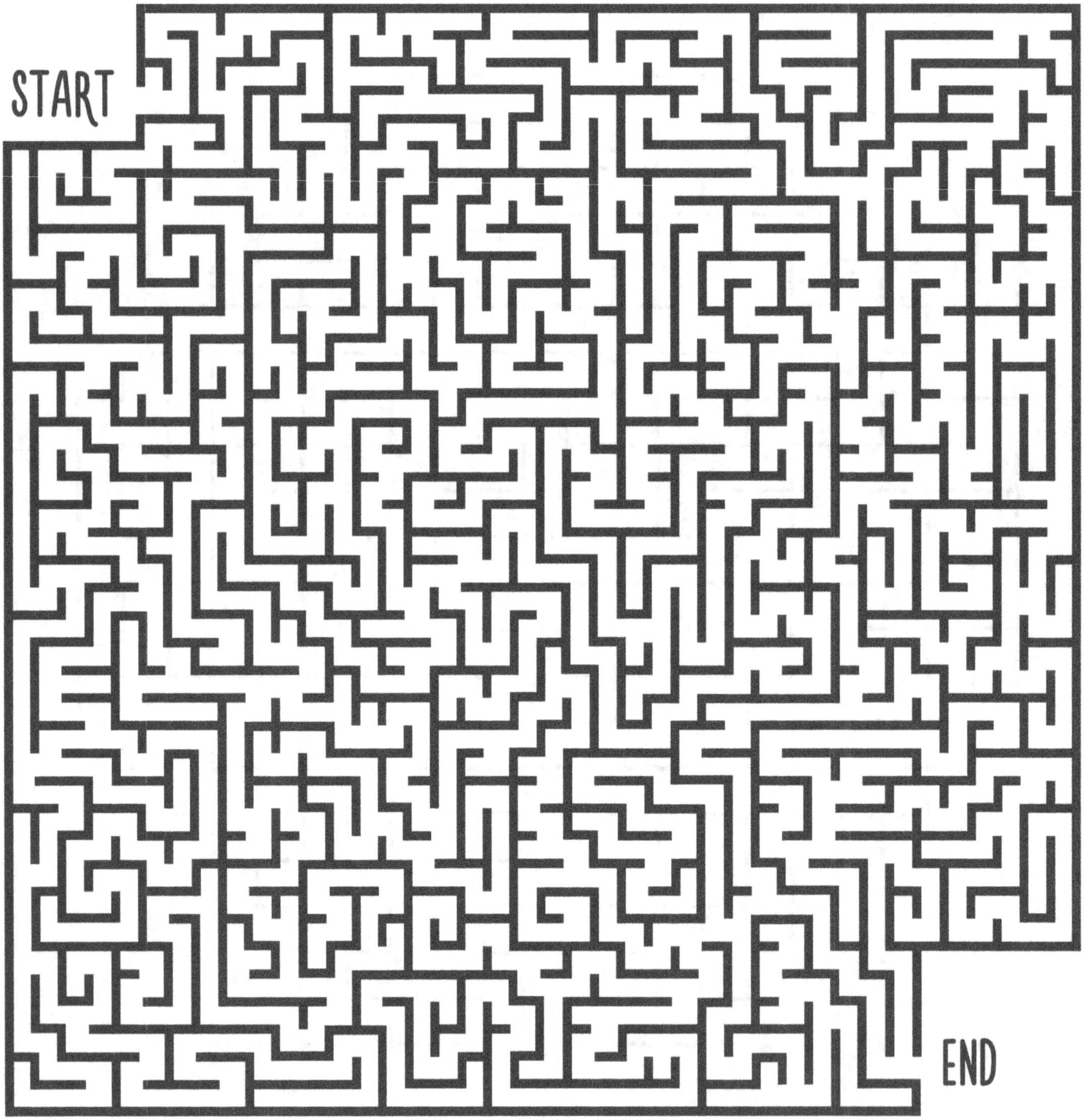

START

END

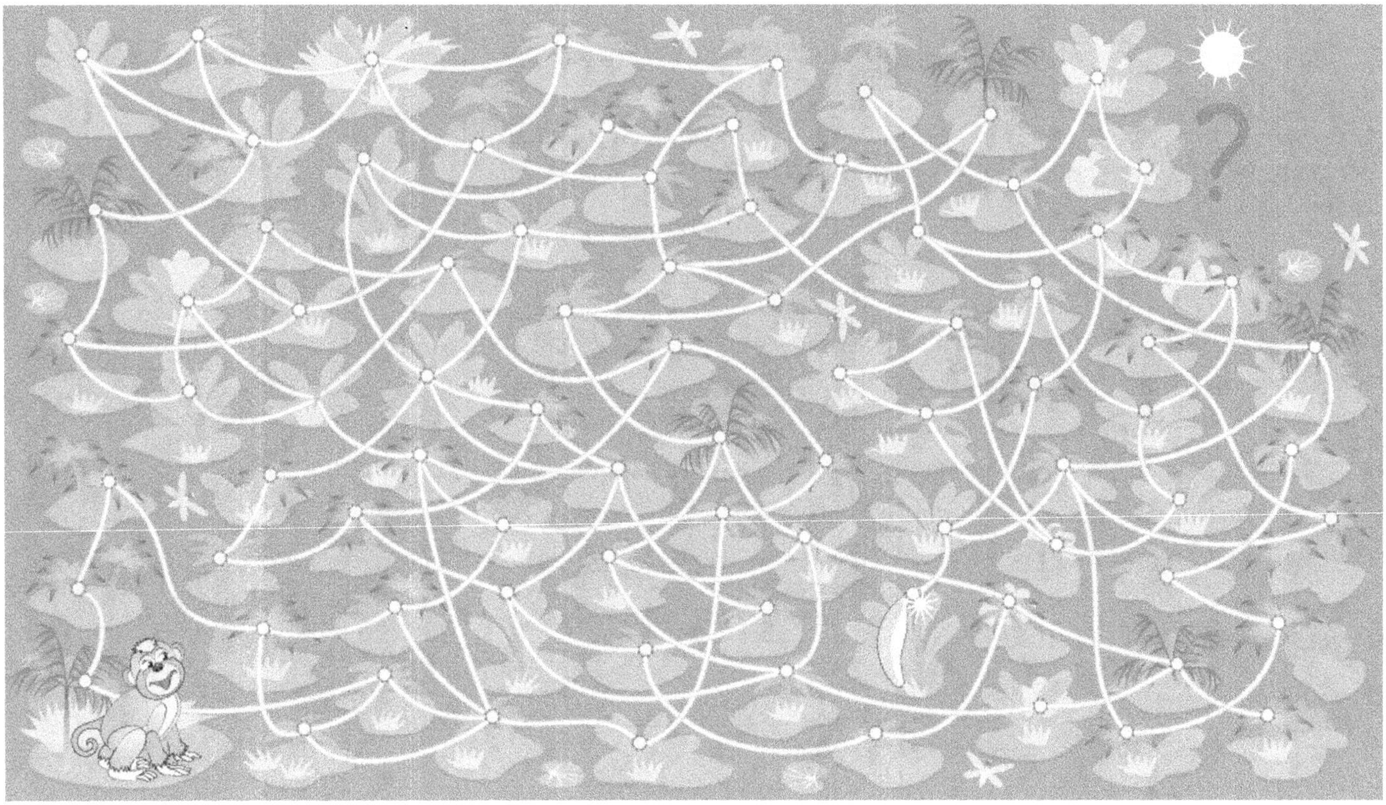

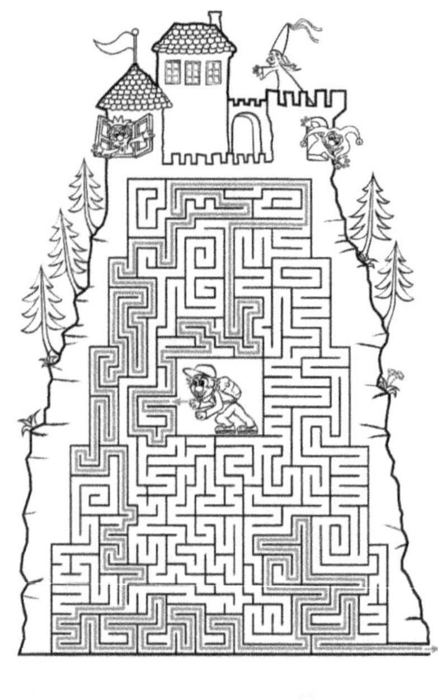
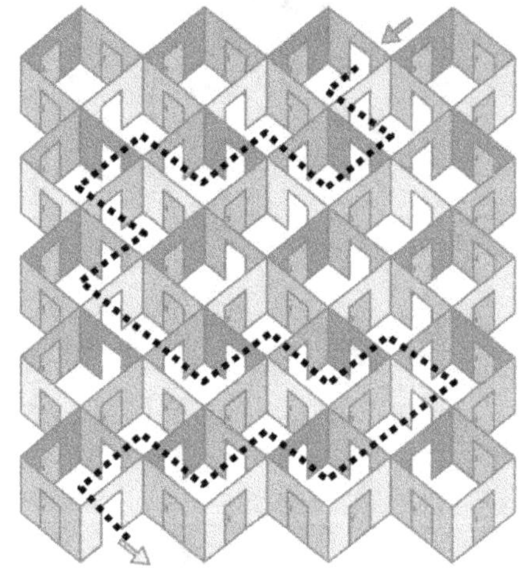
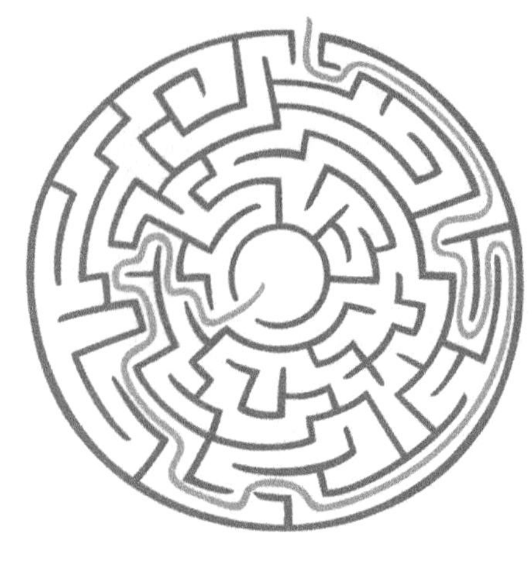
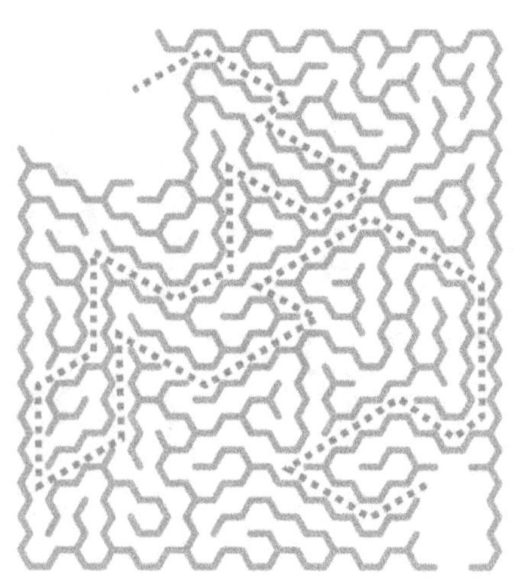
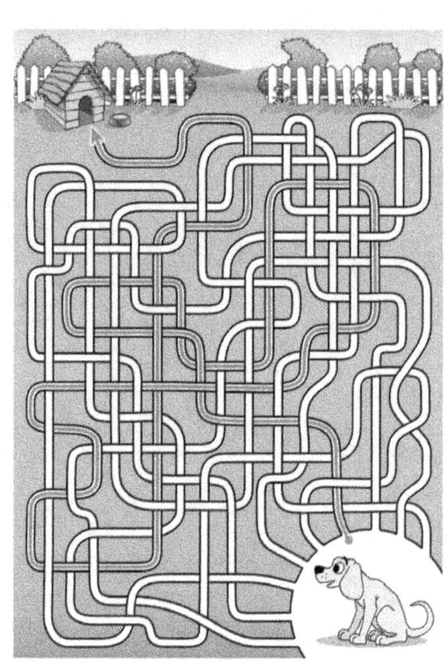
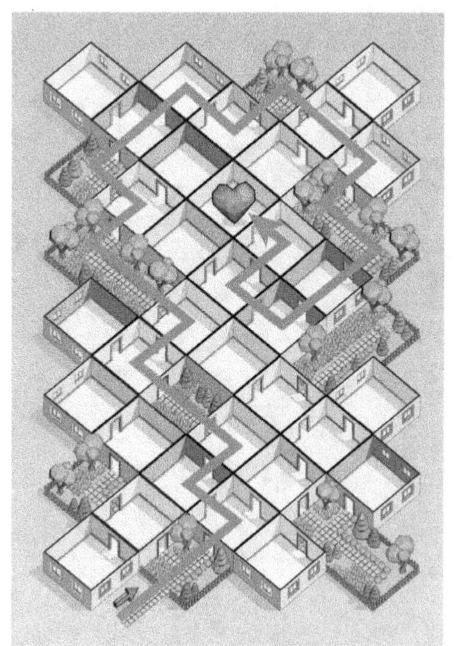
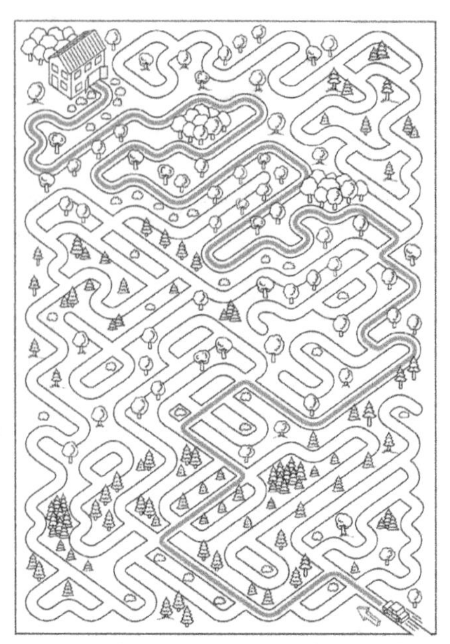
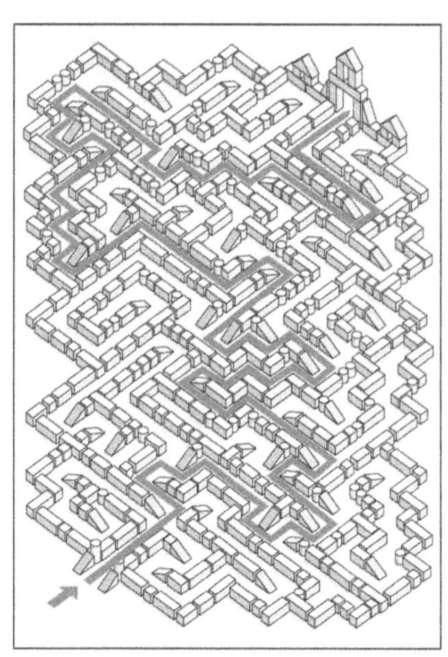
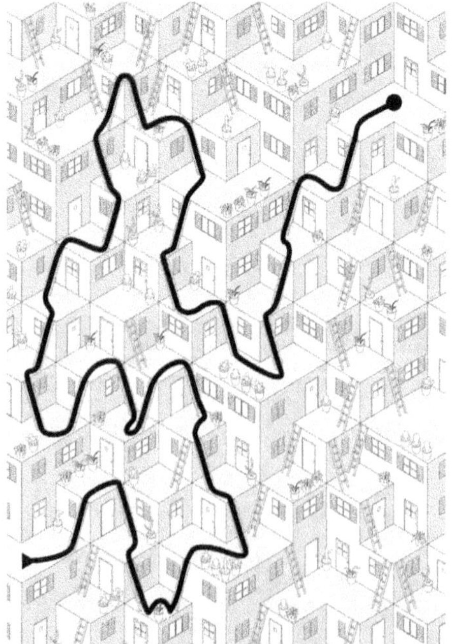

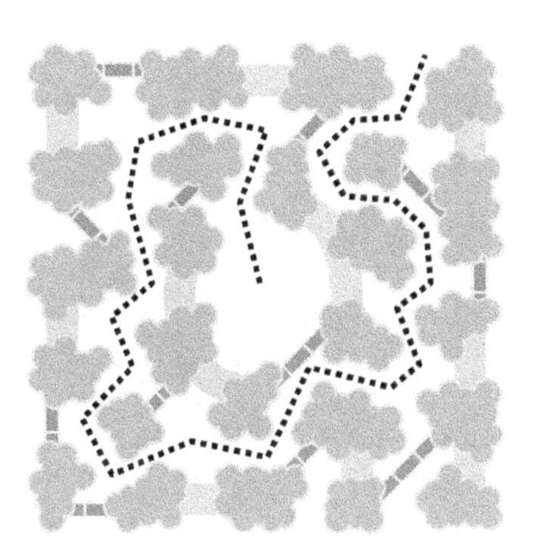
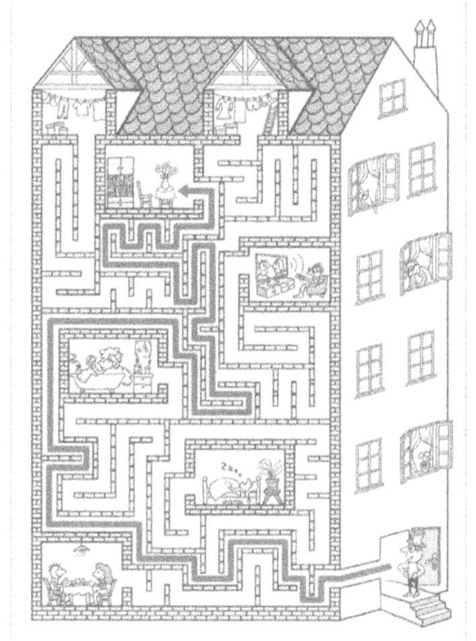
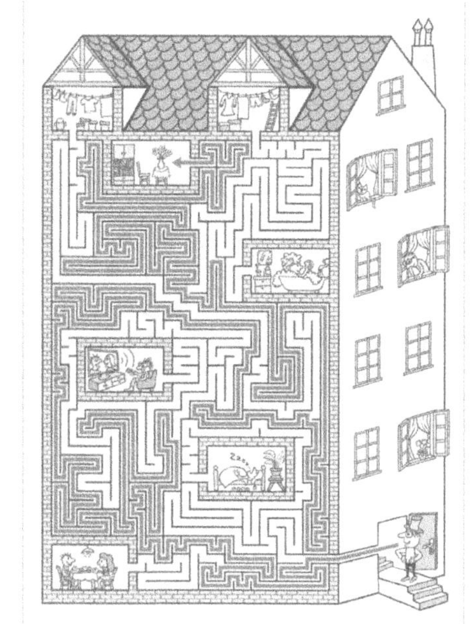
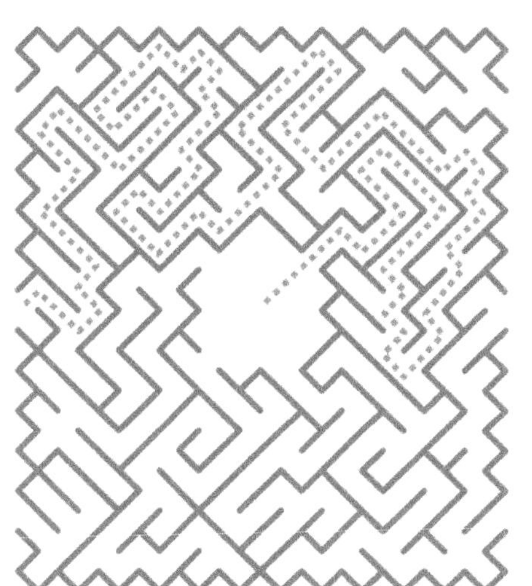
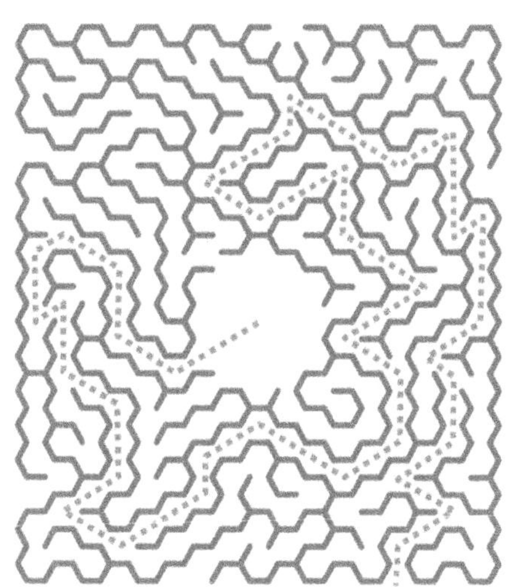
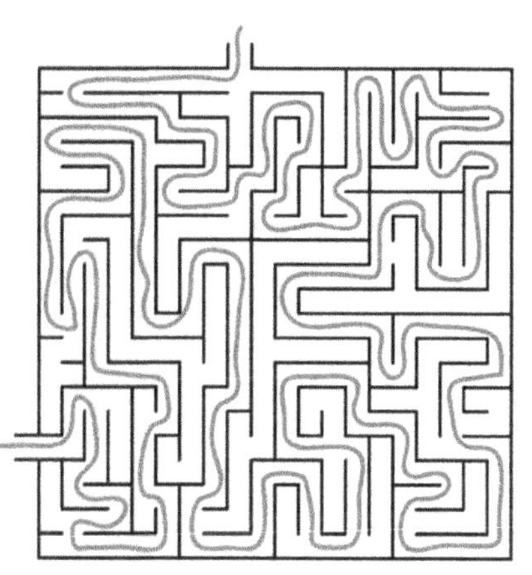
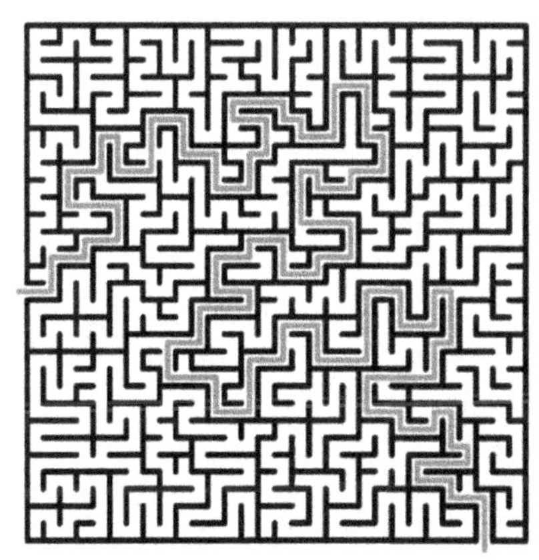
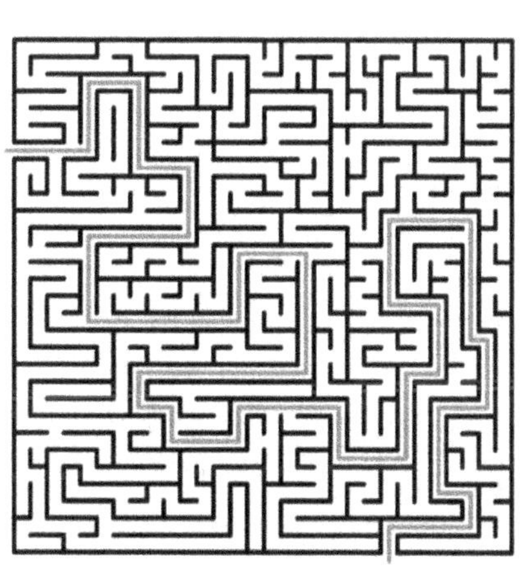
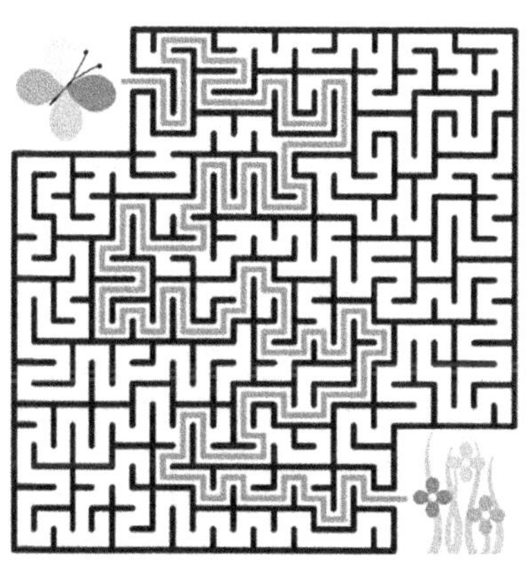

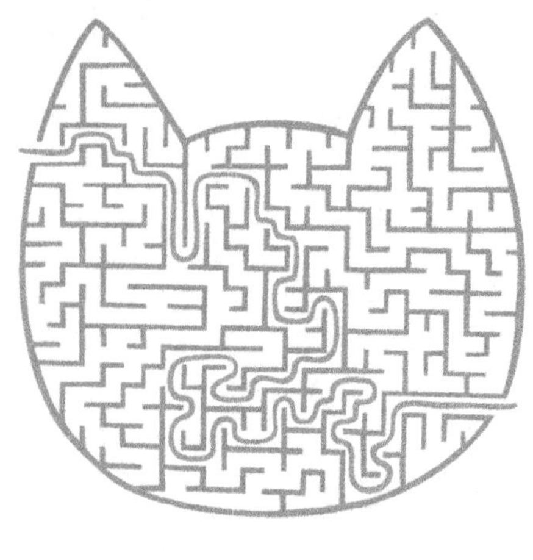
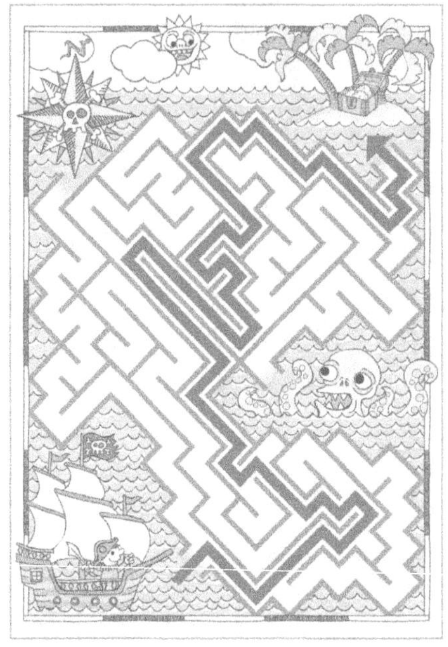
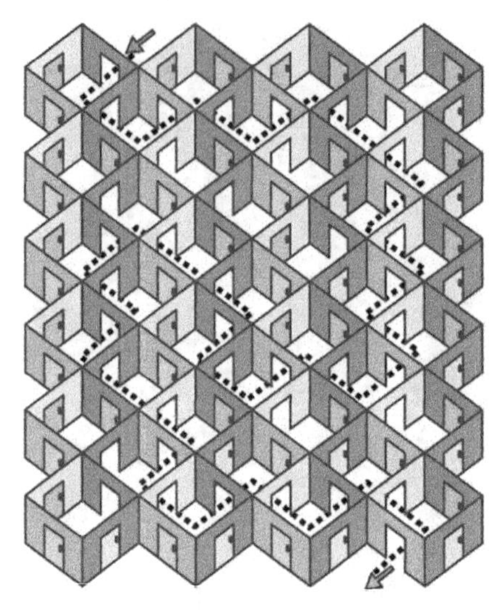
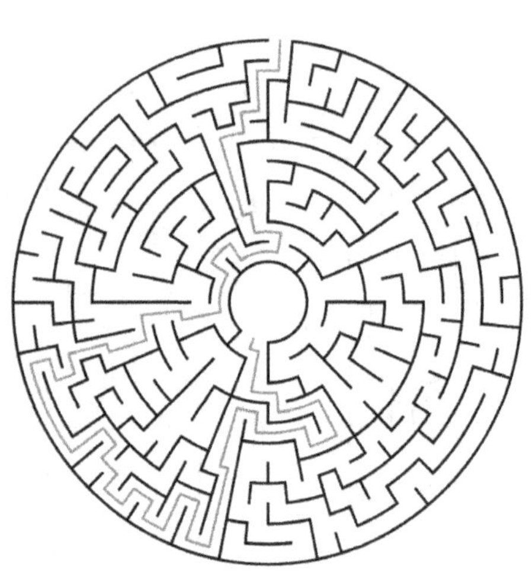
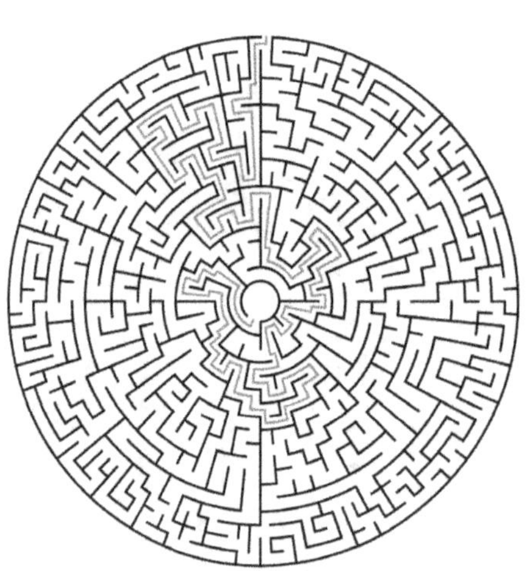
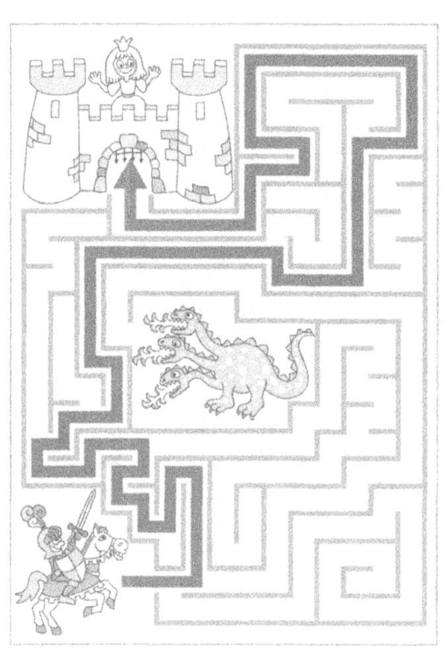
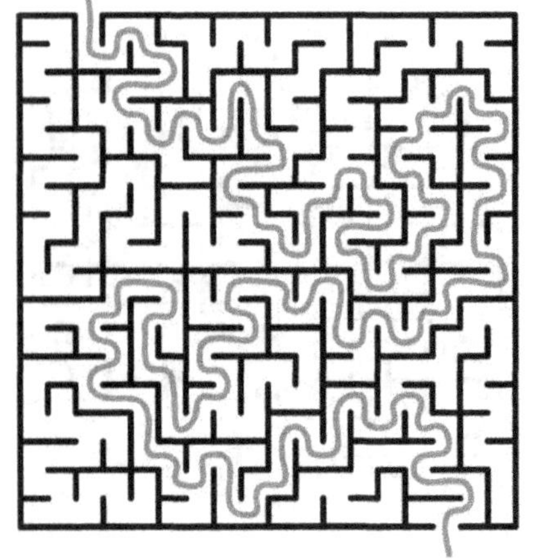
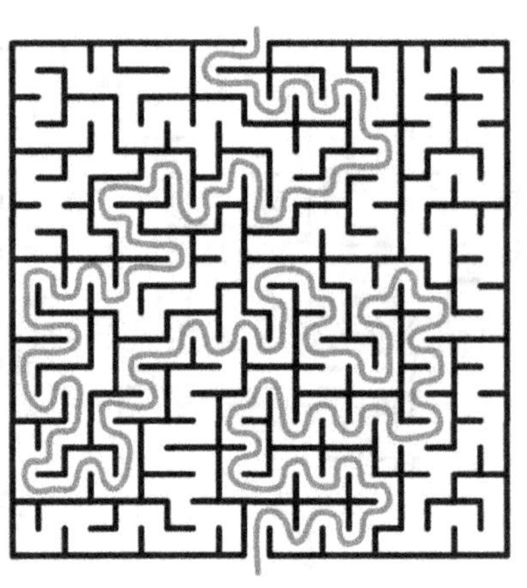
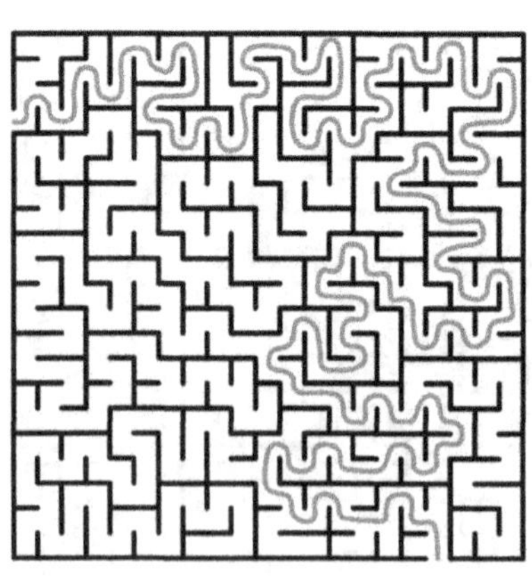

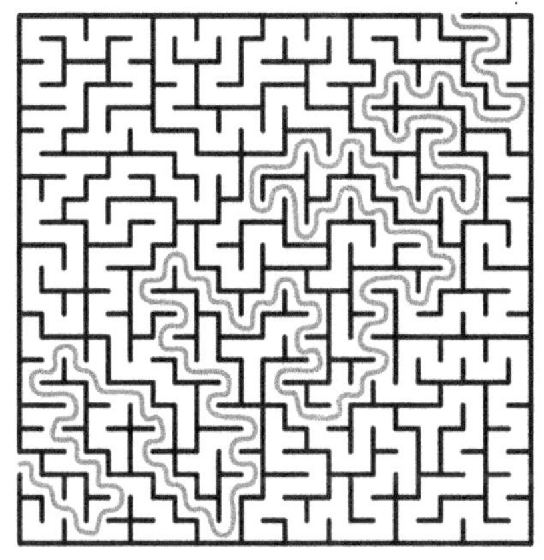
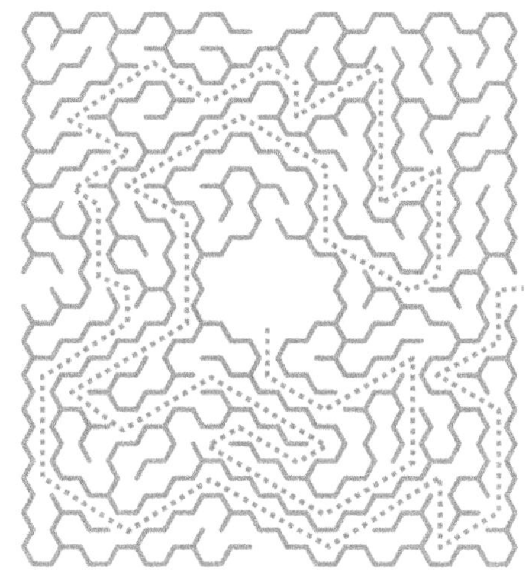
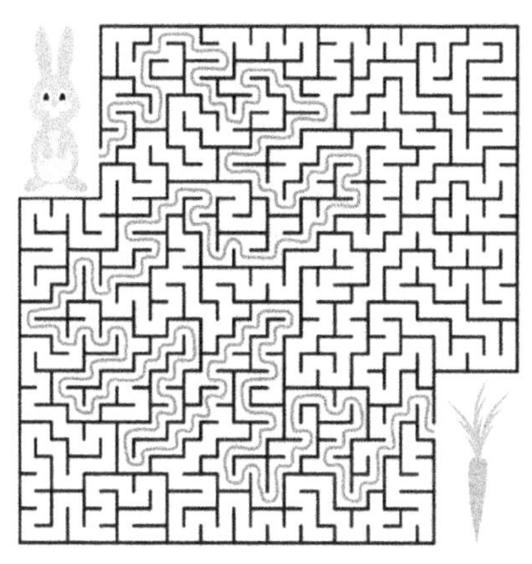
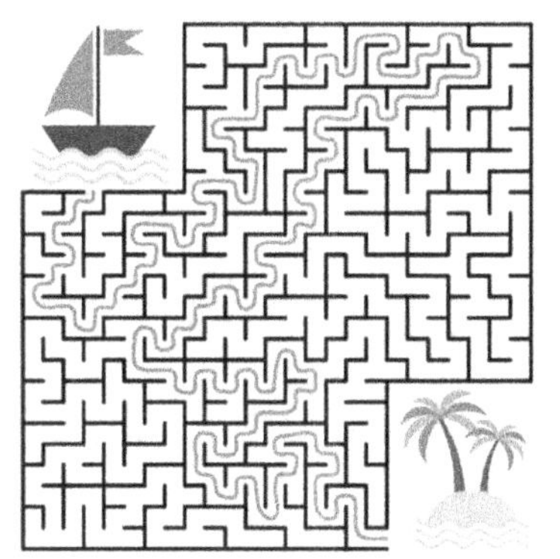
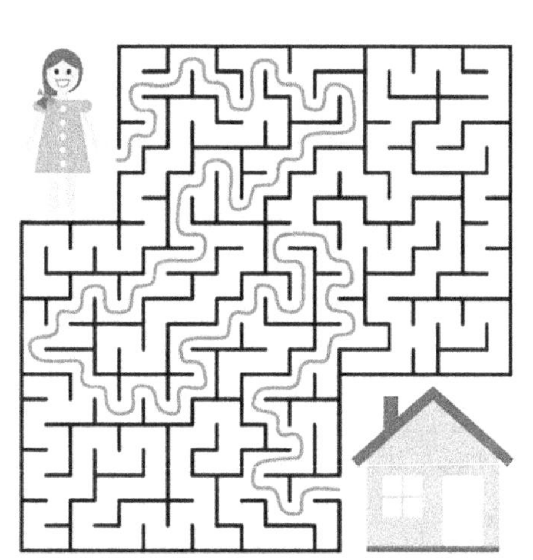
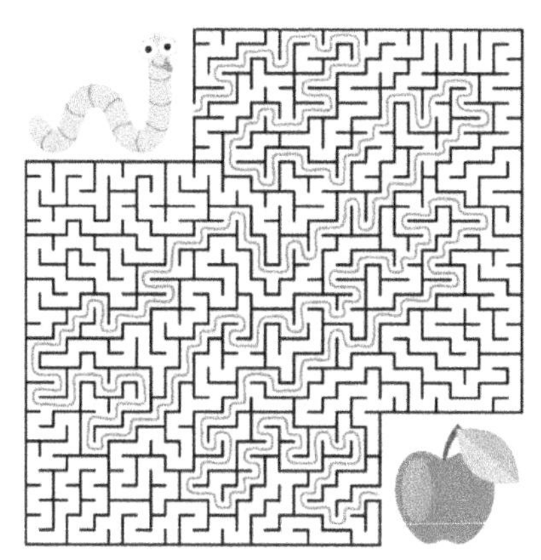
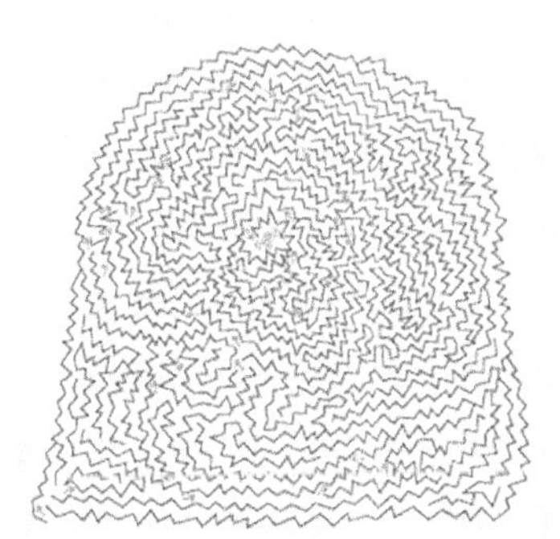
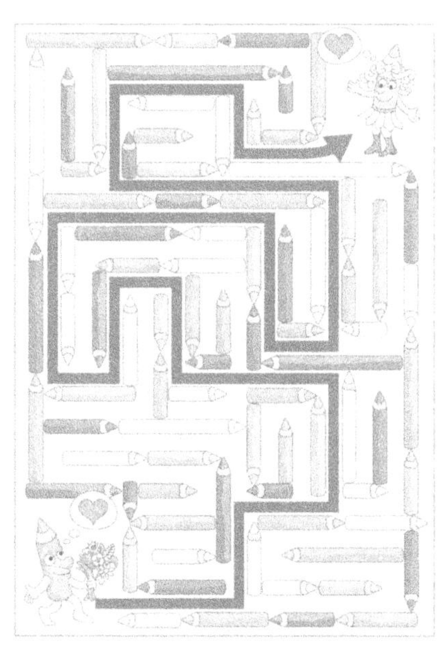
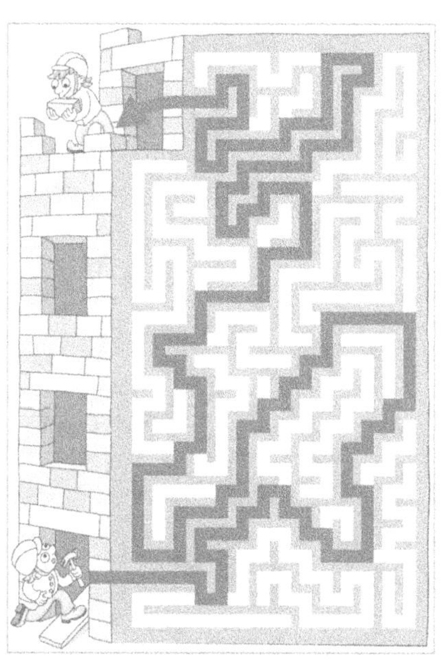

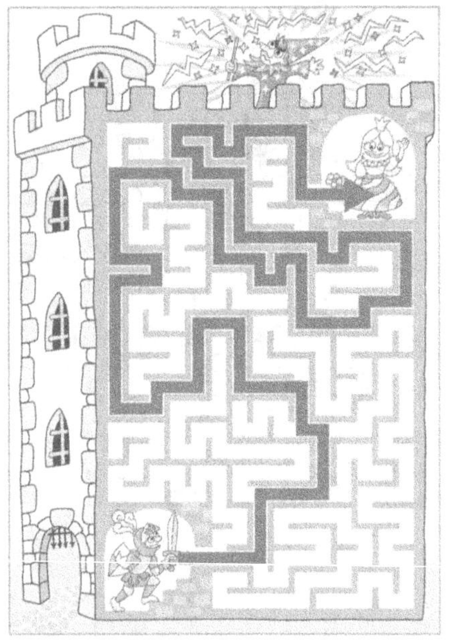
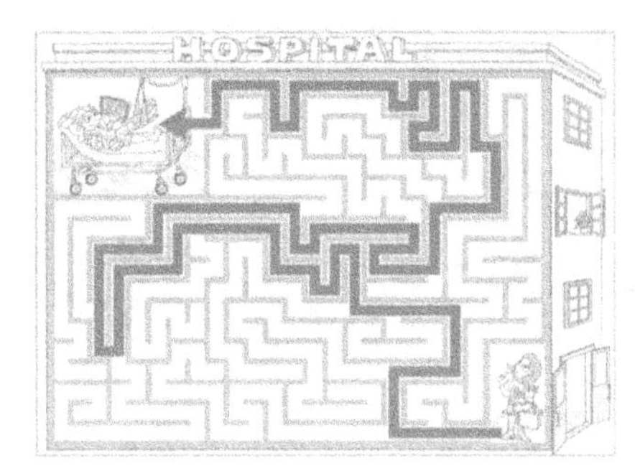
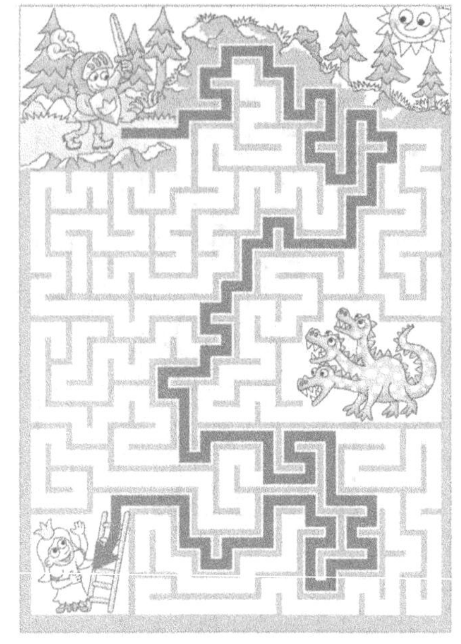
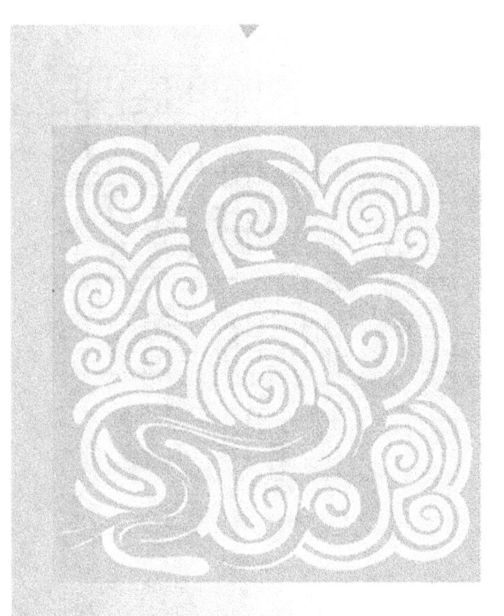
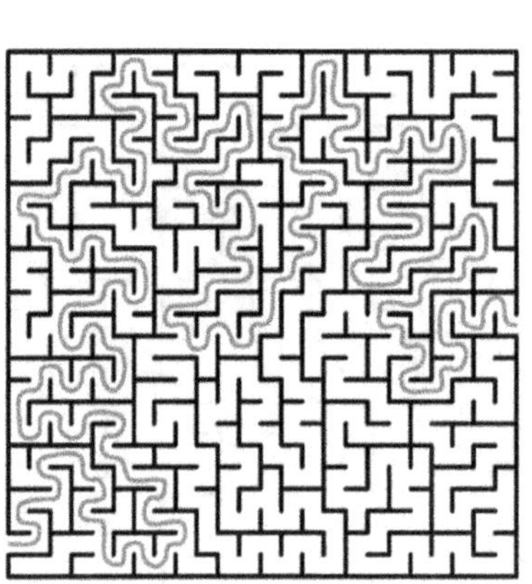
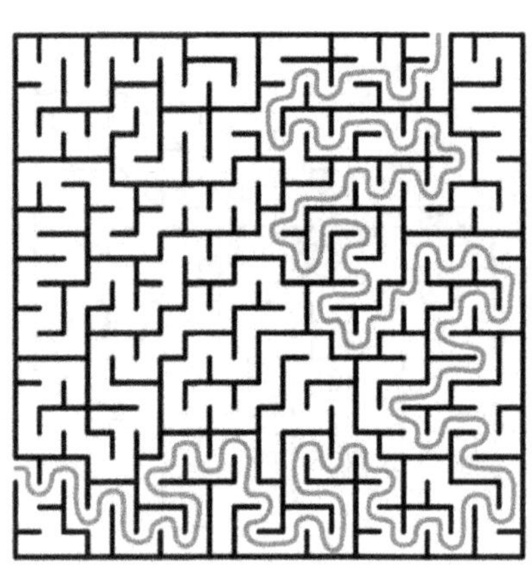
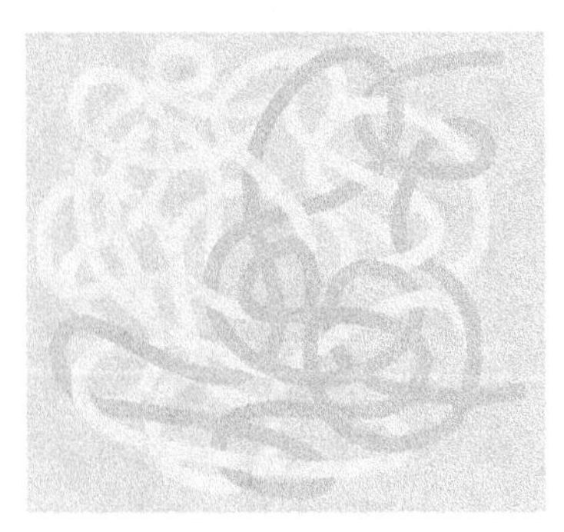
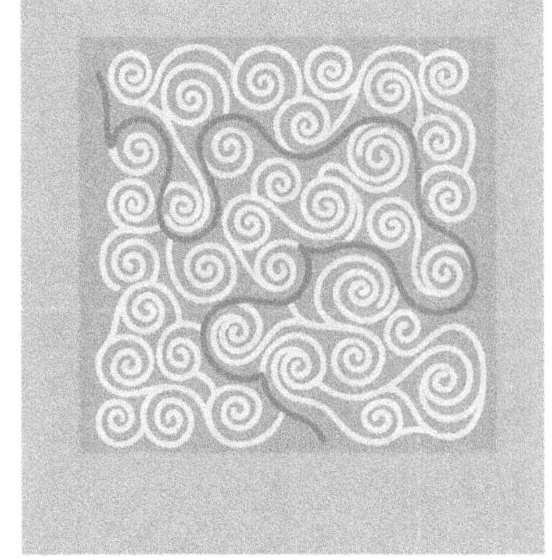
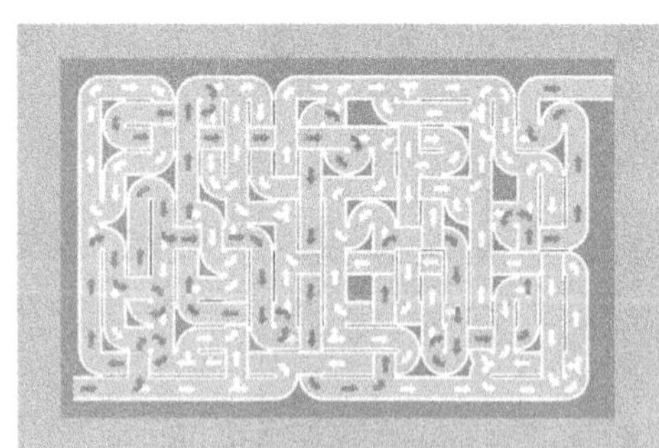

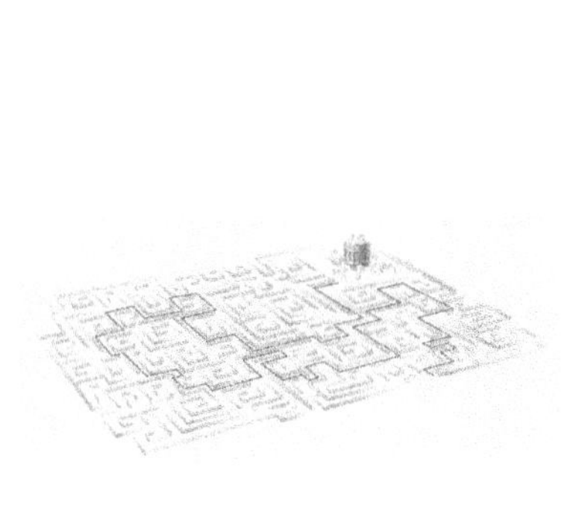
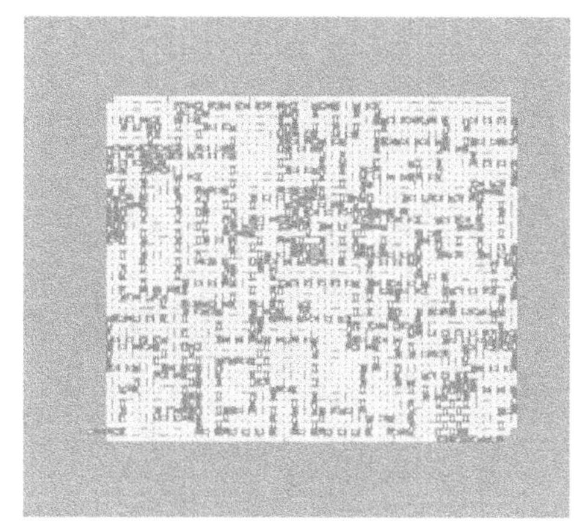
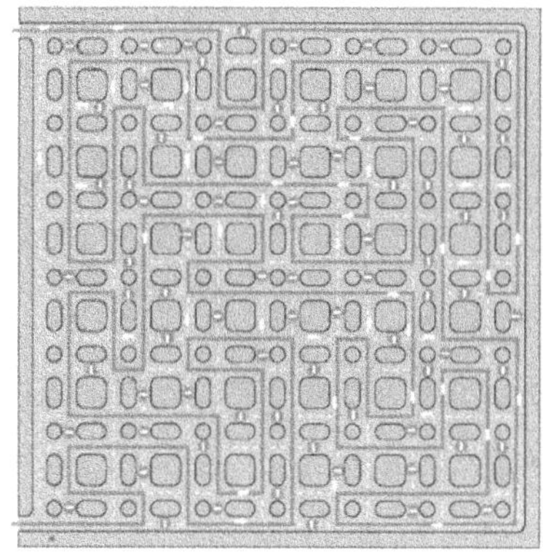
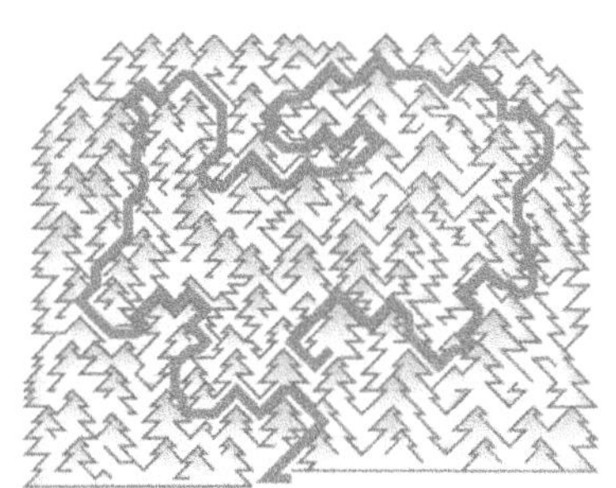
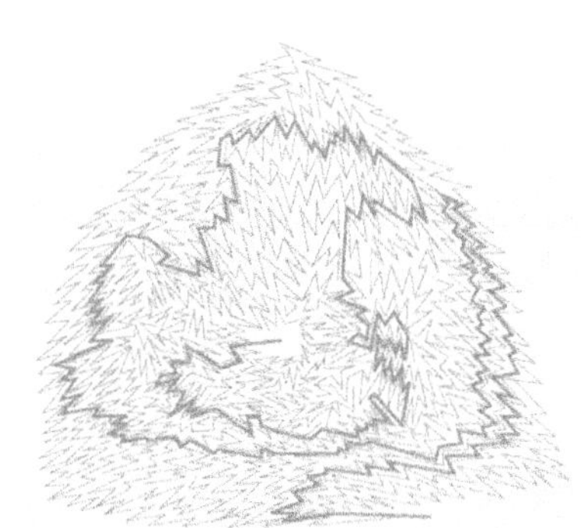
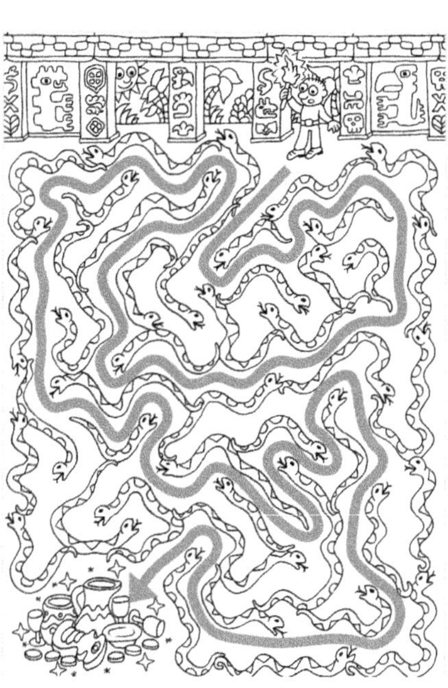
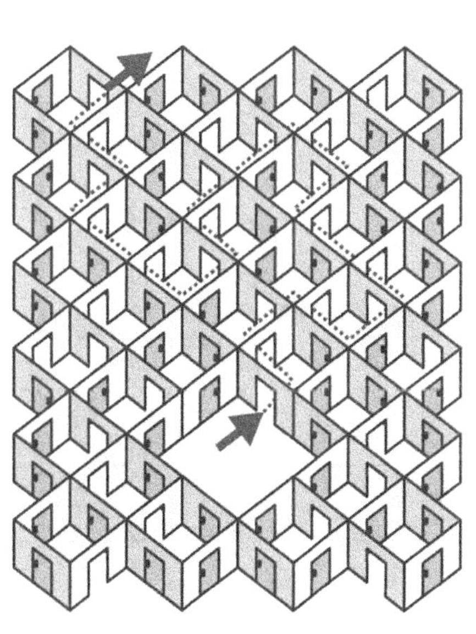
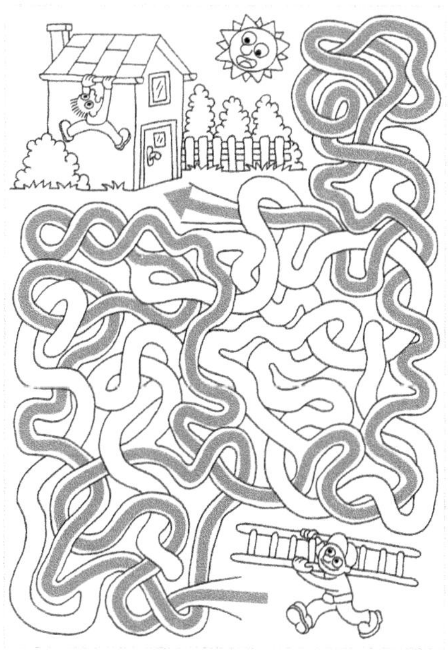
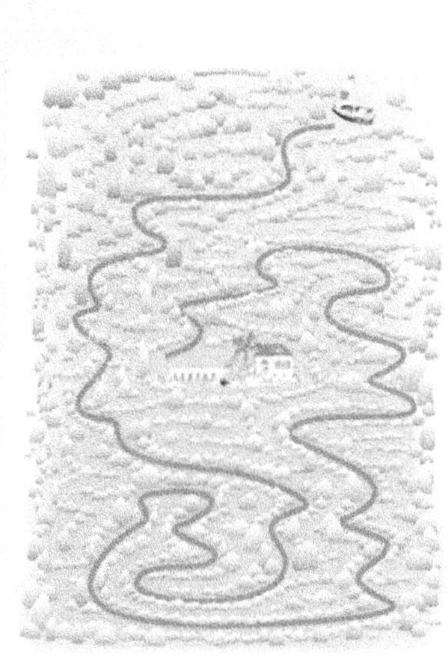

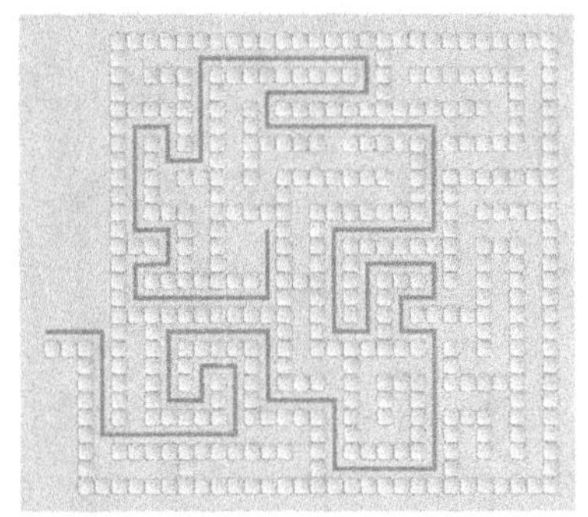
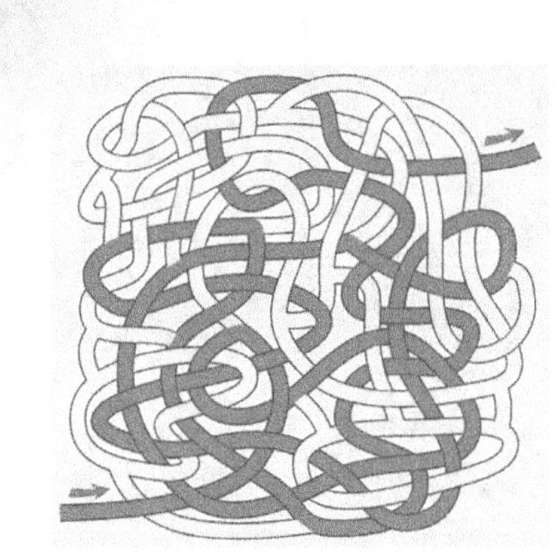
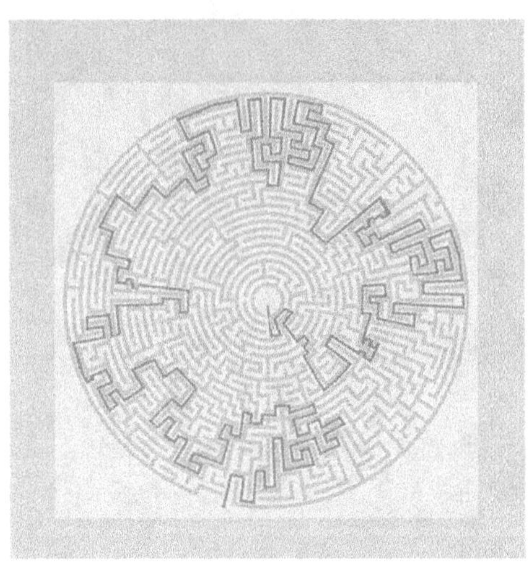
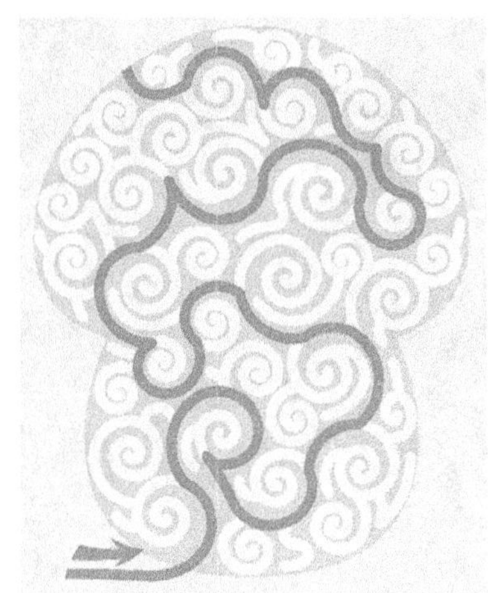
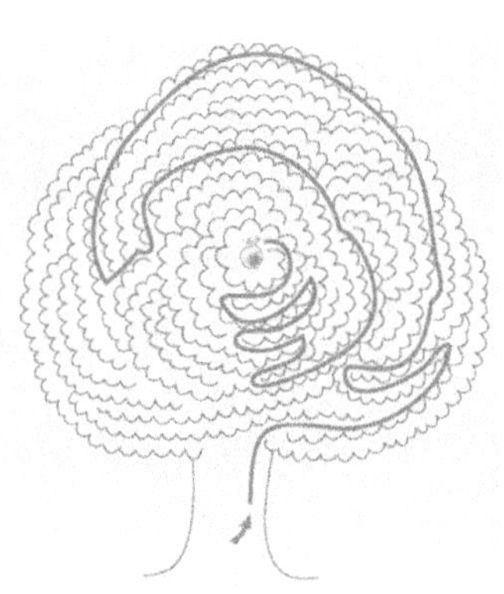
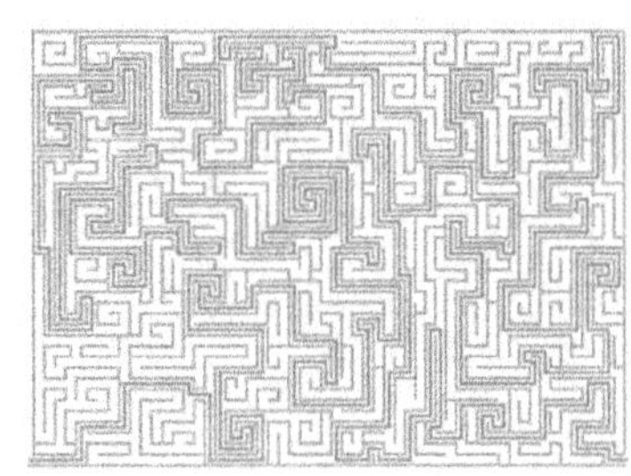
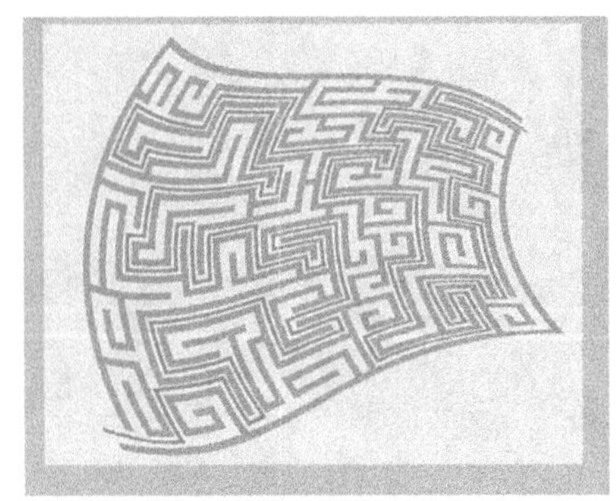
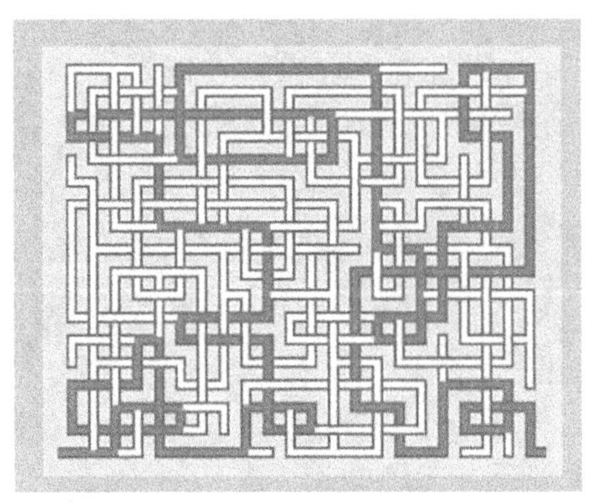
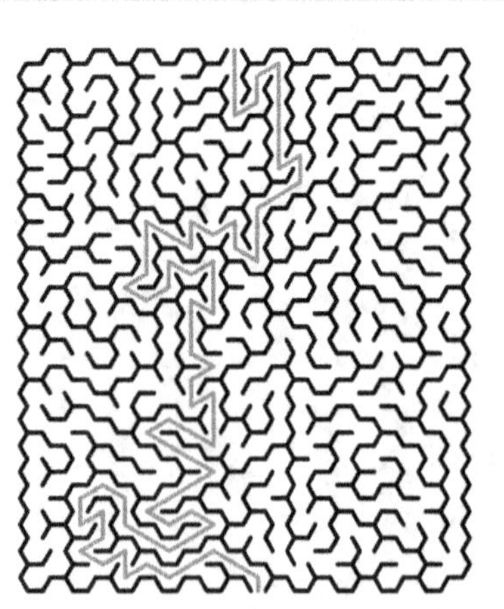

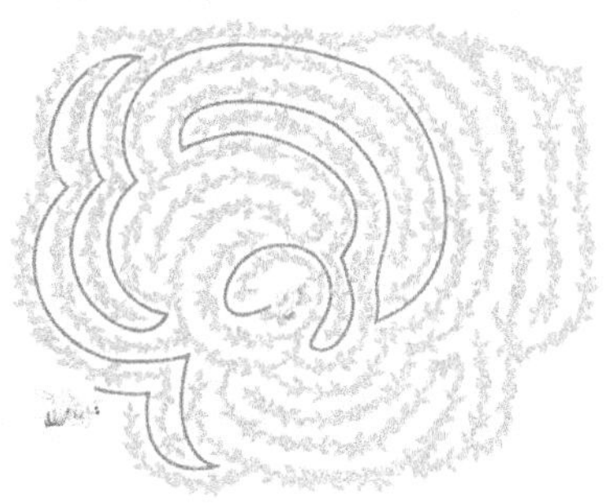

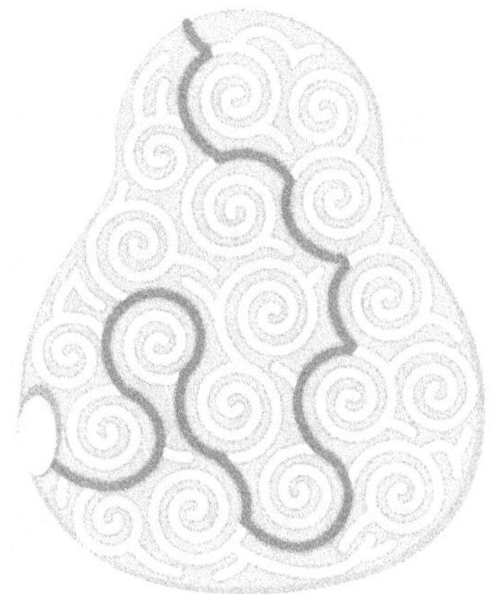

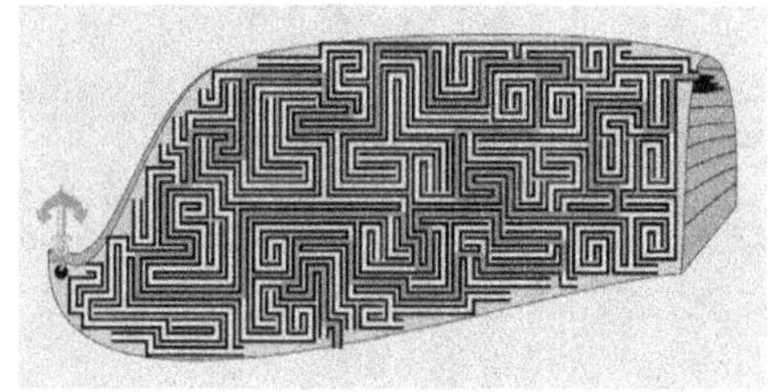

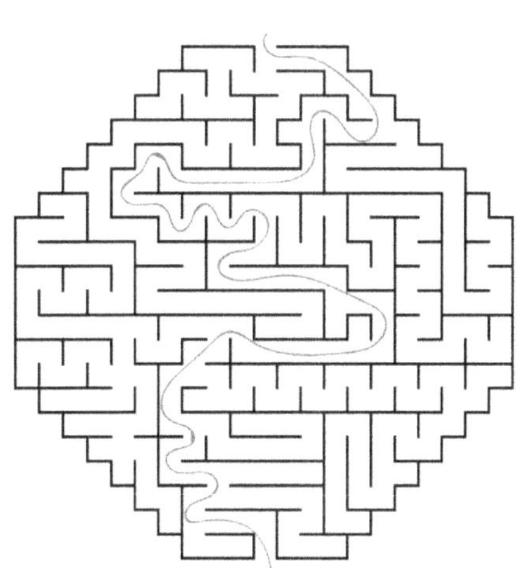

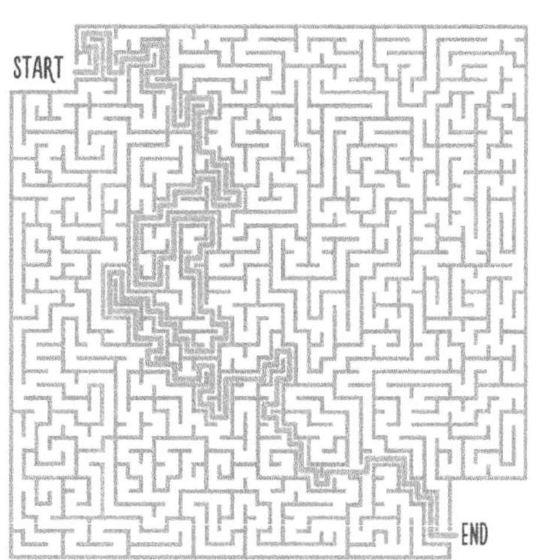
START
END

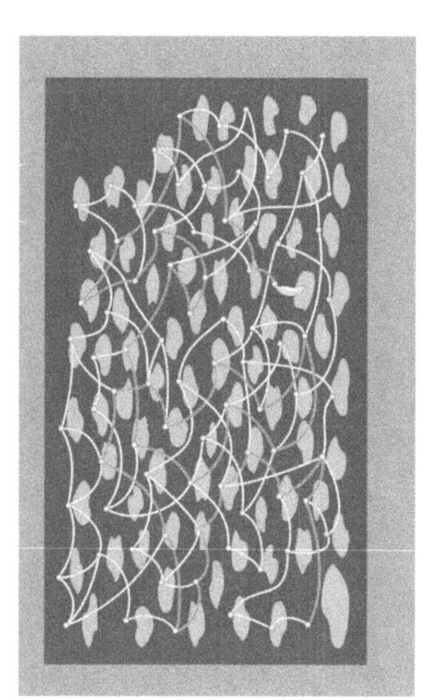